The Santa Po̶̶̶ ̶̶̶ ̶̶̶ ̶̶̶
To Drag Racing

Copyright: Crispin Driver

by Graham Whitehead & Stuart Veitch

Get a Grip...

A **WORKING** BOOKS IMPRINT

First published in Great Britain in 1996 by **Get a Grip...** in association with **The Santa Pod Raceway.**

Get a Grip is a **Working Books Ltd** imprint
3 Quadrant Court,
Middle Street,
Taunton,
Somerset,
England.
TA3 6DQ
Tel: +44 (0)1823-334994
Fax: +44 (0)1823-334897
Email: working.books@dial.pipex.com

A CIP catalogue for this book is available from the British Library.

ISBN 0 9524346 2 8

Project Co-ordinator: David Hayward.
Assistant Publisher: Mary Richards.

Statement from the authors: "We would like to thank everybody who has helped us — you know who you are. We're afraid there are too many of you to list here and the publishers wouldn't give us any more space. Thank you once again. Happy racing & enjoy the book".

Tip-top origination from Graphic Ideas, London. N1
Printed and bound in Spain by Artes Graficas Toledo S.A.
D.L.T.O: 548-1996.

Contents

Foreword

As you develop your skill, and work on your machine, you may begin to go faster, and wish to get promoted to a faster class, or risk getting disqualified for being too fast!

Drag racing takes place along a measured quarter mile of straight track. Two vehicles compete to be the fastest to accelerate from one end to the other. 'OK', you ask, 'if it's that easy, why the book?' Well, it's not always that easy. If that was all there is to it, the team with most power and, therefore, most money would probably win everything.

To prevent this eventuality the racers are divided up into a variety of different classes. To a large extent, classes are defined by how fast you can go. If you usually go slowly, you race against other drivers of similar speed — frequently with a handicapped start. As you develop your skill and work on your machine, you may begin to go faster and wish to get promoted to a faster class, or risk getting disqualified for being too fast!

Eventually you may reach a level where it is the fastest competitor who wins. But there are still limitations on each class — such as engine size, or type of fuel. It is these differences which we will unravel for you. In the following chapters we will explain the basis of each class, and the particular restrictions for running within it.

As each chapter unfolds you will also be led progressively through selected technical features, gradually advancing in speed, until you reach the 'Sportsman' classes and move on to the 'Professional' classes. Finally, you will reach the ultimate drag racers; the Top Fuel Dragsters — not so much a car but a ground-based missile. Read on and enjoy.

Drag Racing

Drag racing did not start as a sport. Naturally nothing this much fun can have had a legal origin.

1971. Freddy White.
Competition Altered.
Bantam Body. 392 ci.
Copyright: Drag Racing News.

In the United States, during the great depression of the 1920's, someone had the brilliant idea of banning alcohol. The theory, as I understand it, was that sober people work harder. In practice a whole new industry was started making, and selling, illegal alcohol. This proved unpopular with those who had made it illegal in the first place, so they tried to catch the hard-working sober people. As the authorities chased faster so the Moonshine boys made their outwardly innocuous runabouts faster still, by hiding bigger and ever more highly tuned engines inside. The Hot Rod was born.

Later, after a wise person had made alcohol legal again, the Hot Rodders, always a lively bunch, had nothing illegal, great fun and very popular to do. However, man is a competitive animal and soon, all over America, quiet back roads were being used to settle the 'mine is faster than yours' argument. But many more people could appreciate these events if they happened in a town. Most towns had a main road running down the middle and junctions controlled by traffic lights. Ideal! Race down the main drag from one set of traffic lights to the other — drag racing.

Legalisation and Organisation

By the late 1940's, as the dust settled after the second world war, there was a growing interest in all things mechanical and hot rodders were becoming restless again. This was the outlaw period of drag racing history — town folk began to frown about being kept awake all night by motor racing — especially as the nice racers were frequently being hotly pursued by eager gentlemen of the law, with horribly loud sirens.

In an effort to become semi-organised, racing moved to dry lake beds such as Muroc, or El Mirage. Unfortunately, as the cars usually raced several at a time, safety soon became a hazard because only the leaders could see where they were going. The next step was a progression to Bonneville Salt Flats in Utah. A national speed week organised in 1948 was a qualified success. Although some racers were being enticed off the road, many more were drawn on in their efforts to emulate those they had seen compete.

The Southern California Timing Association (SCTA) was among the first to try to organise drag racing. Their efforts were not always well received; those not connected with the sport objecting to the seemingly rebellious lifestyle. However, with the approval of the California Highway Patrol and Pomona Police Chief, Ralph E. Parker, the SCTA succeeded in organising a drag race on an abandoned air strip just outside Santa Barbara. When a dedicated drag strip opened in Santa Ana, legitimacy was not far away.

Soon groups of hot rodders got together all over the US and made use of these disused airfields. Here they could race each other off the public highway, away from prying eyes and without attracting unwelcome attention from the law. A measured race distance of one quarter mile, giving ample room to safely slow down before the end of the track.was soon agreed upon. (Although some races are still held over an eighth mile, where running to the quarter would prove hazardous for the particular track concerned).

The launch of Hot Rod magazine, in 1949, was instrumental in the organising of drag racing. In 1951 its editor, Wally Parks, formed the National Hot Rod Association (NHRA) and the serious racers were drawn to the purpose built strips. The illicit street racing continues (in fact thrives) even today, both in the United States and in Europe, but it is the organised sport that is the interest of this book.

When the NHRA banned the use of the superfuel Nitromethane in the 1960's, the American Hot Rod Association (AHRA) came onto the scene. It got a serious grip on the sport when one of its re-organisations separated Nitro Funny Cars into a class of their own in the late 1960's. In the 1970's, Don Garlits formed the Professional Racers

Sept., 1982. Dave Gibbons. Competition Altered. Small Block Chevrolet. 331 ci.

Copyright: Roger Gorringe

1964. Allan Herridge.
Buick Straight 8 Dragster.

Association. It has since folded but the International Hot Rod Association (IHRA) has been more successful and continues today world-wide. Fortunately, Nitro was soon re-legalised and is now used by racers with both Associations.

There are now some 250 active drag race strips in the USA and over 20 in Canada. The sport is growing in Australia, Scandinavia, Japan, Germany and the UK. Interestingly, the German Drag Race Association was originally formed by US military personnel stationed there during the 1970's. In the UK there are three active drag race strips; Melbourne Aerodrome near York, Shakespeare County Raceway (formally Avon Park Raceway) at Long Marston and Santa Pod Raceway, Northamptonshire. Occasional events are also run in Wales, North Weald (just north of London) and along Brighton seafront.

UK Racing History

There is a case for suggesting that drag racing originated in Britain, albeit admittedly a weak one. It would appear that (authorspeak for 'I can't find any hard evidence that...') cars used to race over a standing start quarter mile along Blackpool Pleasure Beach in 1936. It took another quarter century before drag racing became organised nationally. The British Drag Race Association (BDRA) was formed on September 1st, 1960, following an appeal in Car Mechanics magazine to unify local Sprint clubs and run meetings at Duxford, Graveley and other disused airfields. In 1964 the BDRA, led by Chairman Sydney Allard

Sept., 1979. Santa Pod Raceway.
US & European Funny Car
Line-up prior to eliminations
at World Series Event.

Sept., 1980. Paula,
team member to driver
Russ Carpenter, puts traction
compound in front of
the rear slicks of 5.5 ltr
Daimler Dragster.
It ran high seven second
passes at 160mph.

An artist's impression of the proposed layout of Santa Pod. Taken from Drag Racing magazine, December 1965, courtesy of Jeremy Cookson.

(the founder of the Allard Motor Company), and in conjunction with Wally Parks of the NHRA, organised the now legendary Drag Fest at Blackbushe. Starring the American Commandos Drag Race Team, a group of such luminaries as Don Garlits, Buddy Cortines, Danny Ongais and Tony Nancy brought California to Hampshire, having travelled over on the SS United States. In glorious sunshine, the atmosphere was electric. Tommy 'TV' Ivo, who took around eight seconds for the quarter, amazed the 20,000 plus strong crowd as they watched the first serious Nitro run in the UK. They had never seen anything like it.

Who knows, we might still have regular American Commando tours to this day had it not been for the fickle British weather that caused the following year's Drag Fest to be a washout, the tour a financial disaster and ended hopes of it becoming an annual event as planned.

Santa Pod

At the British Hot Rods Association AGM on Sunday October 24th, 1965, a new organisation known as National Dragways announced it would establish a drag racing track at the old Podington Airfield near Wellingborough, Northampton. RAF Podington had been built during the second World War, like so many other airfields now converted to drag strips. The track was named Santa Pod, after the Santa Ana strip in America, and was an ambitious project as can be seen from the illustration of the time shown on page 11.

In 1968, following extended public debate, the BDRA and BHRA merged to form the BDR&HRA. Throughout the seventies the BDR&HRA and Santa Pod Raceway were synonymous, although the club name was shortened to revive the BDRA name in 1981.

Nineteen-ninety was a time of many changes. The BDRA moved their meetings to Avon Park at Stratford and merged with the NDRA to form the British National Drag

May, 1979. Dick Taylor. Competition Altered. Austin Ruby. Pontiac Engine 6557 cc.

Copyright: Roger Gorringe

Race Association, BNDRA. (Rumours by those not involved that it stood for B**locks, No Drag Racing Again have been strenuously denied). Santa Pod changed hands and racing was organised by the Santa Pod Racers Club (SPRC). Early in 1996 Santa Pod Raceway was purchased by a new consortium, headed by Keith Bartlett (ex-president of the ETFA). Keith promoted and developed the European Top Fuel Series throughout Europe between 1991-1994. The new owners intend to invest heavily in the facility to improve its image and appearance in an attempt to attract serious corporate interest. It appears that Santa Pod Raceway is finally in the hands of owners who understand drag racing.

Aug., 1986. Alan O'Connor. Super Gas. 1948 Ford Anglia with a Chevy motor.

Avon Park Raceway

The NDRC was formed in October 1969, first as a sub-division of the BDR&HRA called the Drag Control and Timing Association and then as an offshoot of its' own. It ran its' own competitive meetings at a variety of venues such as Blackbushe and Radlett, but it was not until May 10th, 1980, that their own permanent strip was opened on the runway at Long Marston aerodrome, near Stratford-upon-Avon, Warwickshire. In fact, racing had started on a temporary basis at long Marston on September 9th, 1973, and the track had occasional use annually prior to 1969, albeit in the opposite direction to that in use today.

The NDRC only just made the opening night; when the local ATV television crew needed footage for that night's news the Armco was still not finished. The crowd had started to arrive, the PA was rigged but there was, as yet, no timing equipment. Nevertheless, Russ Carpenter, suited up, climbed into his car Glacier Grenade and the shot was in the can. About two hours later the official opening and racing started at the UK's newest track.

The club changed to the NDRA in the early eighties and the track took the name Avon Park Raceway in 1988. In 1991 David Riswick, the owner of John Woolfe Racing, headed

Aug., 1978. Peter Lantz.
Top Alcohol Dragster.

Copyright: Roger Gorringe

Copyright: Roger Gorringe

July, 1979. Ross Carpenter
in full race apparel
challenges Andrea,
Miss Santa Pod Raceway,
in a model dragster race at
the Brighton Dragster &
Custom Show.

1970. Clive Skilton.
Top Fuel Dragster.

Copyright: Roger Gorringe

the investment of some £500,000 in a new track surface and other major improvements. The money came, in part, from the Burton Tailoring family with whom he had family connections.

In 1992 major changes were made to the club and track. The NDRA was dissolved and replaced by APIRA, the Avon Park International Race Association. Stratford-on-Avon council refused planning permission for the development of the facility and issued an enforcement order limiting the use of the land to 14 days of motor sport a year. That has led to major upheavals; the construction of the Acoustic wall, the movement of the pits and other work intended to bring the facility up to NHRA standards.

Although direct involvement by the NHRA in Avon Park Raceway has been ruled out for the time being, the changes should enable a representation of the planning application and hopefully grants for extended use will be made available in the near future. For the 1996 season the owners of Avon Park have entered into a joint venture promotion with Keith Bartlett's Real Racing Management Ltd (RRM) to promote three events, including the inaugural FIA European Professional Drag Racing Championships in Top Fuel and Top Alchohol. RRM plan to promote racing at Avon Park raceway in 1997 ensuring both cross management and promotions at the two main UK race tracks.

Oct., 1979. Sammy Miller poses with Andrea, Miss Santa Pod Raceway, in front of Funny Car line-up before eliminations.

York Raceway

Aug., 1988. Liv Berstad. Top Fuel Dragster.

Racers in the north of England felt a bit out of it in the sixties. The likes of Steve Murty with his blown 1000 cc Vincent and a minibus load of colleagues called themselves the Pennine Drag Racing Team. In 1974 they realised their dream of their own track when they opened Crossland Moor near Huddersfield. Ten thousand people turned up at their first two meetings. However, this didn't outweigh the 12 complaints apparently received by the local council and the planning permission was revoked. The club hastily moved two 1975 meetings to Aintree racecourse in Liverpool. Although well attended, they were not a financial success.

It took until June 1977 to find, inspect, acquire and transform the disused Melbourne airfield. Steve 'Murt' Murty and his wife, Leone, formed Pennine Promotions, managed to raise the finance (again) and the dedicated few set about the potholes with spades and barrows. The PDRC may not have had large resources at their disposal but they had an abundance of enthusiasm.

The New York Raceway ('New' was added in 1979) still hosts six meetings a year, including one national IHRA points round. The raceway was able to benefit from some of the ex-Open Golf Tournament seating also installed at Avon Park in the early 1990's. It deserves to have better attendance of both competitors and spectators.

Safety

Drag race legend Don Garlits believes that the parachute is the single biggest safety feature on a dragster, "I've had a few not open, crashed every time".

Safety is a primary concern in all forms of motorsport, but none more so than drag racing. The most obvious and, for the spectator, the most frustrating, safety implication is that drag racing stops when it rains. The smallest amount of moisture on the racing surface will cause a dramatic reduction in tyre grip. There is no point in merely changing to rain tyres; the whole set-up of a drag race vehicle is based on its getting maximum grip and it simply cannot be de-tuned to run in the wet. There are many more aspects of safety in the sport, all with the well-being of both the spectator and competitor in mind.

Parachutes and Fire Suits

Safety equipment for use on cars and bikes, such as mechanical parts and roll cages, is available from a wide variety of sources. When is comes to Fire Suits, Parachutes and safety blankets, there are only two front runners; Simpson and Diest. Although there are some areas of duplication, to a large extent Simpson specialise in protecting the driver and Diest in 'chutes and stopping bits coming out of broken cars.

Bill Simpson, now President of Simpson Race Products, was a racer himself. Allegedly, one day in 1958 his car wouldn't stop; the following day he bought an Army surplus parachute and became the first to use one to stop a dragster. It was Jim Deist, of Deist Safety, however, who became the more involved in parachute engineering. At the time

INDIANAPOLIS MOTOR SPEEDWAY

"I'm sure it helped that I was a driver myself. Not only did I know the other racers, but they understood that the stuff I wore was the same stuff I'd sell them.

Guys like A.J. and Bobby Unser, they always used to bust me.

Anyway, we were at the Speedway one day, and I told them, 'You know, I'm tired of this. Let's go down to turn one. You can pour gasoline on me, and light me on fire.'

So off we went, and of course everybody followed us. Well, there I sat, on a metal chair, and they poured the gas on me. George Snider threw the match in.

Now I'm on fire. And the next thing I see is Johnny Rutherford or somebody standing there, sticking a hot dog into the fire.

Pretty soon after that, every one of those guys was wearing my stuff."

46

Bill Simpson demonstrates his faith in his fire suits. (This advertisement reproduced by kind permission of Simpson Race Products).

he worked for Irving Air Chute (who make drogue 'chutes for 'planes). When approached by a racer who knew this, he provided an old 'chute from a Lockheed 94C. It had to be the heavier duty 'plane type; that for a skydiver would have ripped to shreds the instant it was deployed. After a little development (to make sure it didn't catch on the back of the car), it worked fine. As other racers saw it working, so they wanted one. Irving were not really interested in the business — drag racing still had that 'tacky' image — so Diest Safety were born.

In 1963 Jim Deist developed the first aluminised asbestos fire suit. It was able to protect a driver for around 10 seconds; which was enough at the time. As speeds climbed and exposure times with them, suits got thicker to compensate. But that made them bulky.

Bill Simpson was a friend of Apollo 13 commander Pete Conrad. During a discussion between the two, Bill had the inspiration to develop a suit made out of Nomex, the kind of material used for the space capsule parachutes. This material now forms the basis of suits worn by the majority of drivers in every form of Motorsport worldwide.

Top Fuel drivers are typically protected by Nomex underwear, socks and balaclava. On top of this would go a five-layer Nomex and Kevlar fire suit. Either special shoes for dragster, or boots for Funny Cars protect the feet. Hands are covered with multi-layer Nomex gloves. The driver's head is protected by a helmet incorporating a neck-sock, that would be tucked inside the neck of the fire suit. Less explosive classes are protected by reduced specification clothing, but the principle remains the same. The level of confidence Bill Simpson has in his product is shown by the picture on the introduction page of this chapter.

Almost every competitor we have seen uses a Simpson Helmet. In the same way that there are minimum specifications in each class for safety suits, so each grade of helmet must meet a minimum specification. These are laid down by the Snell Foundation (named after a racer who died when his helmet failed). The Snell Foundation test samples of all types of helmet, and only when one has the appropriate Snell certificate is it suitable for use in that category of racing.

As a Funny Car pops his 'chute at Santa Pod, the finish line can be seen behind him, and the chase/fire truck. From the back of the truck the Fire Diver, Peter Thompson watches intently. His fire suit was given to him by Funny Car driver John Spuffard; John knows that the quality of Peter's suit may be of benefit to him one day.

Safety Safari

The NHRA use the name Safety Safari; Avon Park call them FAST, the Fire and Accident Safety Team; Santa Pod just refer to them as 'The fire marshals'. Call them what you will, these are the people whose job it is to keep racing safe — even when it goes wrong.

They get drivers out of wrecks or fires. They put out fires. They watch for things happening that should not, such as oil or water leaks. They clean up the oil or water after it has leaked. If possible, they dry off the track after the heavens open or after they've cleaned it. On a good weekend they simply sit and watch the racing. A bad weekend may give them nightmares.

A typical minimum team for a top meeting would be;

- Two in a chase vehicle/fire engine behind the start line,
- One in each lane at the start line.
- Two in a chase vehicle/fire engine by the finish line; one of these fully fire-suited, able to dive into a fire and get out the driver,
- A fire engine 200 yards beyond the finish line.

In addition there will be an ambulance (or two) available, with paramedics at both ends of the track, and a doctor. RAC regulations specify the minimum amount of cover for each category of race meeting. For example, racing cannot proceed without an ambulance present. If the only one is taking an injured idiot, who got drunk and fell into the toilet, to hospital, racing has to wait until it returns.

General Safety Regulations

There is a set of general regulations that apply to all racers, irrespective of class, and some of these are documented here such as, all vehicles must pass a Technical Safety inspection before any runs are made. With the progression to faster and more powerful classes additional, more stringent regulations, are applied; a selection of these are documented as part of the introduction to each class chapter.

Air foils
Once adjusted, must not be moveable.
Alcohol
Any driver found to be under the influence of alcohol will be disqualified automatically from the event and possibly future events as well.
Arm restraints
Mandatory in all open topped cars. They are wrist straps that will hold the drivers arm within the car in the event of an accident and hence reduce injury.
Ballast
Where weight is added to bring the car's weight up to the class minimum, or to improve the weight balance, it must be solid, permanently fixed to the car's structure and not extend behind the rear of the body, or above the height of the tyres. Recommended types of ballast include heavier gauge steel floors or additional safety equipment such as roll bars or flywheel shields etc.
Batteries
A maximum of 2 batteries, both of which must be securely mounted outside the passenger compartment. Elastic straps are not allowed.

Bodies

Regardless of class, all cars must have some sort of body additional to any frame structure surrounding the driver and extending to the firewall. Bodies should be constructed to keep all parts of the driver free from the wheels, tyres or exhaust.

Brakes

Brakes must be in good working order and not excessively lightened. With the exception of Street cars running slower than 11.50 seconds, brakelines must be routed outside the frame or enclosed in a thick walled steel pipe where they pass the flywheel area.

Breather catch cans

All breather pipes must vent into a catch can to prevent spillage of liquids.

Clothing

Throughout practice and racing, it is mandatory for a driver to wear a crash helmet and clothing as specified by the RAC MSA or higher as specified for the class requirements.

Clutch

Each clutch equipped car must be fitted with a foot operated device to enable the driver to positively disengage the engine from the final drive.

Computers

Only computers installed as original equipment on stock vehicles are allowed. Data recorders may be used, so long as they do not activate any function of the vehicle. No devices activated by the tree, the timing lights or the radio are permitted.

Deflector plate

The plate must be installed on rear engine cars between the roll cage and the engine. On any enclosed engine/driver configuration a full bulkhead must completely seal the driver from the engine (firewall).

Driveline

Where the driver sits over or behind the differential, he must have a protective shield. Where an open driveshaft is used, a driveline loop should be fitted near the front u-joint to support the driveshaft in the event of failure. This is also generally mandatory in most classes where slick tyres are optional. As soon as

The 'Lower Engine Ballastic Restraint Device' part-fitted. More often than not called a Diaper — it catches the bits when the bottom end bursts and is a mandatory requirement on Top Fuel cars.

the greater grip tyres are used, a loop must be fitted to the driveshaft. Open drivelines passing any part of the driver's body should be enclosed in a steel tube fixed to the frame.

Engine

Crankshaft centreline to be within 24 inches of the ground. Engines with press-on front pulleys or dampers should have these drilled and bolted.

Exhaust

All cars to have exhaust headers and collectors that direct gasses out of the body and away from the car, driver, fuel tank and tyres.

Fire extinguisher

To be fitted in all cars, within reach of a driver in the normal strapped in position. Any car capable of faster than 9 seconds should have an installed fire system with nozzles aimed at the engine and driver.

Flash shield

Carburettors must have a flash shield covering the top, back and sides to prevent fuel being siphoned into the airstream or blown into the driver's face.

Floors

All cars must have metal floor pans or sub floors, with suitable drain holes so that liquid cannot collect and create a fire hazard.

Flywheel/clutch

Heavy duty or explosion proof are highly recommended. All cars with a clutch must have a covering for it and the flywheel. There is a very large amount of energy in a fast rotating flywheel and a great amount of power controlled by the clutch. Failure of either is usually catastrophic and it is vital to contain the resultant explosion. The IHRA rule book has seven pages of very specific rules applicable to flywheel shields (bellhousings) and clutches.

Frames

Each chassis built to Minimum Specifications must be inspected on its first outing of each calendar year, and the current year log book must be carried with the car.

Fuel system

Fuel lines near the flywheel (except in Street cars slower than 11.50 seconds) must be protected by steel tubes. Those near a supercharger should be

The Burst Plate on the inlet manifold of a Top Fuel engine is designed to rupture in the event of an explosion and prevent the launch of the supercharger.

protected against the belt breaking. Fuel tanks and lines are to be outside the driver's compartment and sealed from it. Lines are not permitted in the transmission tunnel. A locking fuel filler cap is required and safety fuel cells are recommended.

Harmonic damper

Fitted to the front end of the crankshaft (frequently doubles as fan belt bottom pulley), to damp out torque pulses and reduce flexure in the crankshaft. Production types are not robust enough for hard race use, so aftermarket race bred types are specified for most faster classes.

Hub caps

Must be removed.

Ignition

A positive on-off ignition switch, or magneto kill switch, clearly marked, should be within easy reach of the driver.

Jack and stands.

Cars should always be supported by more than one jack when being worked under. Disregard of this rule is grounds for immediate disqualification.

Master switch

A master cut off switch, clearly marked, must be located on the rear of the vehicle and stop all electrical functions.

Neck brace

Mandatory for all cars running quicker than 11.49 seconds.

Nitrous oxide

An N_2O sticker must be displayed near the bottle, that should be securely mounted outside the driver's compartment. Many rules apply to the safety of the installation and its operation. It should only operate at full throttle.

Parachute

Mandatory for all vehicles quicker than 9.99 seconds, or faster than 150mph.

Reverser

All cars must be fitted with a reverse gear in full working order.

Roll bar/cage

Where class regulations insist on a roll bar or cage, there are very specific stipulations about the construction. All open topped cars require a roll bar.

A flywheel/clutch housing tested and certified for compliance with the appropriate safety standard: SFI spec 6.2.

A transmission safety blanket, fitted over the reverser on a Top Fuel car.

The N$_2$0 safety label is still required near the bottle, even when the window is transparent.

Safety hubs

These are rear wheel hubs that are attached to the suspension, with the drive through the middle. If a drive-shaft breaks the wheel stays safely attached to the car. They are mandatory on most top classes.

Seats

Seats must give full back and shoulder support in the event of an accident. Heat insulation is recommended.

Seat belts

Street cars have a minimum requirement of a lap/diagonal belt. Where class rules specify a roll bar or cage, a full harness is required. The minimum is a four anchor point, three inch wide strap type, but five-point is recommended and mandatory for all cars running 10.50 and quicker. For Dragsters, Funny cars and Altereds the harness should have a fireproof cover.

Starters

Push starting, once the most widely used starting method, is not allowed. All cars must be self-starting, either with fitted on-board starters, or by one attached to the car and fed from batteries in a trolley.

Steering

Steering systems will be carefully inspected, especially those fitted to Modified or Altered cars.

Superchargers

All superchargers must have at least two tie down straps to retain them in the event of an explosion. If alcohol or nitromethane fuel is used, a safety blanket (similar to a Flak jacket) and straps are required.

Support strap

A mandatory strap to support the rear of the engine in the event of clutch or flywheel disintegration is mandatory.

Suspension

All Street cars must have full suspension.

Throttle

Throttles must all have positive return springs attached directly to the carburettor, and a stop to prevent the linkage from moving too far and locking

Seat padding Top Fuel style. Basically, it is a heat-proof Flak jacket on the seat.

Engine Ballistic Restraint Devices prevent bits flying into the crowd when something like this happens.

open. For nitro and alcohol fuels, a manual foot-operated return is also required.

Traction bars

These and other devices to transmit rear axle torque to the frame and prevent spring wind up must not be longer than one half of the of the car's wheelbase.

Transmission

Auto transmissions must have positive reverse lock out and a neutral start safety switch.

Transmission shield

It is mandatory for any car with an auto transmission running 10.90 seconds and quicker to have a shield or blanket similar to a supercharger safety blanket covering it.

Wheelie bars

Must have non metallic wheels.

Wheels and tyres

All street tyres must have a minimum of the DOT required tread depth. All cars running quicker than 10 seconds must have an approved racing tyre at the front as well as at the rear.

Windscreens

On any car without a windshield, a fireproof deflector must be fitted to divert wind, liquids and other foreign matter over the drivers head. Windshields must be shatter-proof and clear, except for factory tinted glass.

Window net

Ribbon type window safety nets, to restrain the driver in the event of an accident, are recommended on all full bodied cars and are mandatory for Super Gas, Pro Modified and where specified by class requirements.

Traction

*Drag Racing
is a sport of
acceleration.
The key to
acceleration
is traction.*

Naturally, a racing car is lighter than the equivalent street car. There is no point trying to lug all the extra weight of sound deadening, carpets and four comfy seats etc. up the track. The generalisation is that every 100 lbs of weight lost is worth 1/10th of a second over the quarter mile. Having shed all dead-weight, replaced some of it with safety features like a solid roll-cage and a fire system, and having tweaked the engine a bit, the next task is to make sure that all the engine's power is made optimum use of. Traction is needed.

Watching Street classes is interesting because of the different levels of ability. It is not uncommon to see a Street car sail from the line, with a fraction of the power of a Pro Doorslammer, but with wheelspin and a trail of tyre smoke for the first 150 feet. The difference is that the Street car tyres and suspension are designed for comfort and cornering ability, whereas the Pro Doorslammer type are optimised for straight line use.

Line Lock

A line-lock is a switch, or tap, that is used to lock the brakes at the front of a car. It is used in the Burnout to stop the car rolling out of the water-box.

The driver rolls around the water-box, to avoid wetting the front tyres, and then reverses the rear tyres back into it. He applies the brakes and, while holding brake pressure with the pedal, he applies the line-lock. He can then release the brake pedal and the line-lock will hold brake pressure on the front wheels, leaving the rear wheels free for the burn-out. If he wishes to perform a rolling burn-out, the line-lock is released when the rear wheels are spinning which allows the car to go forward.

Tyres

Street tyres are designed to do everything in all weathers and some do it better than others. Slick tyres have no tread pattern to disperse water, just lots of rubber in contact with the track surface. When it comes to dry weather straight line racing, drag slicks are best. They differ from their other racing cousins, such as those used in Formula One, in that they are designed purely for optimum transfer of power in the forward direction; their side-walls are significantly softer and thinner, and they are usually run at a lower tyre pressure. Here we will not consider front tyres; most of the action is at the back (although special front tyres, based on aircraft technology, do exist for speeds in excess of 200mph).

There are different slick tyres available for each requirement within drag racing. Fast, powerful, light cars like Fuellers and Funny cars will need a different tyre from a steel-bodied bracket racer. In general the heavier car will use a stiffer side-wall tyre, run at a higher pressure. Typical pressures are around 18 psi for bracketeers, five to seven psi for Super Gas, around five psi for Pro Mod, and Top Fuel tyres are between three to five psi). The stiffer wall helps reaction and 60 foot times, moving the bracket car more quickly and consistently. With a heavy car, getting the mass moving is of prime importance.

The more flexible wall tyres on Fuellers help because they tend to wrap-up and cushion the sudden force of acceleration. In addition they have a sling-shot effect that, although marginally dropping reaction time, they reduce ET. Further, the flexible sidewall and tread areas work together to elongate the contact area under acceleration. Examination of such a tyre under power reveals a straight rear edge and surge of rubber at the front as the tyre is pulled off the track and thrown forward. It also allows for tyre growth at high rpm, providing an artificially higher gear ratio.

A Dragster's wheel showing how the tyre is bolted to the rim.

As with all racing tyres a selection of compounds, in a range of hardnesses, are available. Too hard a tyre on a car and it will spin slightly on the run, too soft and there could be too much grip, pulling the engine revs down out of the power-band on the launch. The strip of white shoe polish often applied to the tyre wall is to enable the crew to watch the tyre closely on launch and observe tyre slip should it occur.

Modern drag tyres have a tremendous amount of grip — so much that the wheels can sometimes spin inside the tyre, especially at the low pressures used. That is why wheel rims can frequently be seen with a ring of screws around them indicating that the tyre bead has been screwed to the wheel. The other downside of low pressures and soft sidewalls is that the tyres are only rigid under power. After the finish line cars and, in particular, bikes can be seen weaving and bouncing as they slow. This is not some mysterious braking technique. The drivers can't help it; their tyres have simply gone floppy!

Compounds are stickiest at around 100 degrees Celsius, hence the burnout; but overheating the carcass will also lose grip and shorten tyre lifetime by part-curing the compound. It is this curing and resultant hardening that will usually denote the practical end of the tyre's life, rather than tread depth. Where Fuellers might get around six runs from a pair of slicks and Pro Modified 10, Super Gassers would expect to get 25 to 30. The same Super Gas tyres on a 12 second car would probably last a whole season.

Tyre-Shake

This is a difficult one. The knowledgeable see it happen and talk about it. It is obvious to the driver when it happens; it varies from a mild vibration to a severe shuddering so violent that his eyeballs rattle. However, its' causes are not so obvious. Certainly nobody we asked could explain it to us. Here is our theory. It is probably related to the tyre distortion under power, mentioned above, and the low tyre pressures used. If the combination is slightly wrong, some of those distortions appear under the tyre, as standing waves along the contact patch. If the driver is able to drive through the vibrations, they go away at the higher speed, indicating a link to a resonance effect. But, as the distortions act to reduce the contact area, the attendant reduced traction makes it difficult to continue acceleration. Occasionally a circumstance will arise whereby the crew cannot eliminate the problem by tyre or pressure changes. Then the solution seems to lie in the suspension set-up, reducing the tyre downforce at a particular point after launch. Alteration of that set-up and its relationship to the gearshift points moves the tyre-shake point, and can eliminate it.

It is this close relationship between tyres, suspension and traction that we shall explore next.

Weight Transfer

Not surprisingly, having got the weight of the car as low as possible (within class restrictions of course), what weight is left should be used as efficiently as possible. Invariably the engine is at the front, driving the rear wheels. On launch as much as possible of the car's weight should be on the rear wheels to make them dig in for maximum grip. With a seriously fast Pro class car, it is important to have the lowest possible profile and centre of gravity for sound stability and aerodynamic reasons. But for Street and Bracket racers, it can be a distinct advantage for the car to sit higher than normal, so that the centre of gravity (C of G) is correspondingly higher. Thus when the car is launched, the inertia (that force that attempts to resist a change of movement of a mass) causes C of G to appear to shift towards the rear of the car. This reduces the proportion of weight on the front wheels, with a corresponding increase at the rear.

An example of weight transfer. As the engine is engaged the car's centre of gravity shifts towards the back wheels lifting the heavy front of the vehicle.

With a normal road car, the suspension would work to counteract this effect. For drag use a different arrangement is required and a variety of methods are available. The principle is similar; to make the front end light and the rear end heavy. Altering the front shocks to 90/10's benefits the former. These have differing downwards and upwards resistance; 90 per cent of their capacity resists downward movement, and 10% resists upward. Therefore as the front lifts, the shock stays nearly the same length, lifting

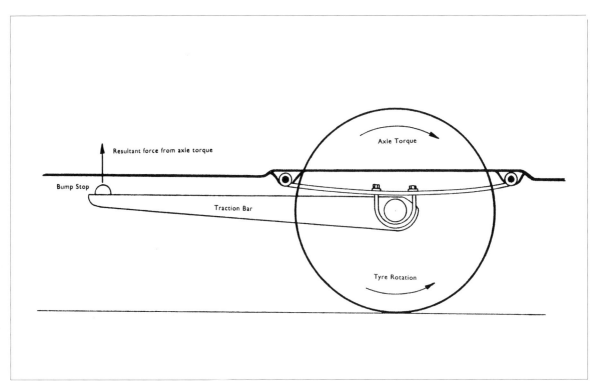

the front wheel, or at very least letting the downforce on it reduce. The 10 per cent bit lets it down gently later. By the way, they are not street legal.

At the rear a firm suspension is a benefit; all that lovely weight transfer we've strained to achieve counts for nothing if it is all taken up in compressing the rear springs. This is especially obvious on drag bikes where, instead of the conventional rear spring/shock arrangement, the rear chassis is simply rigid. With a car there are other ways, which help the inertia-derived C of G shift, by transferring the back-axle torque to the chassis in ways that help the transfer equation.

Traction Bars

Also known as anti-tramp bars, these are fitted to the rear axle to prevent it rotating as the engine torque is transmitted to the wheels. They project forward from the axle and, as it tries to wind up under power, the front end of the bar meets the floor of the car to limit axle rotation. They may have either a rubber stop on the end or be bolted to the chassis.

Ladder Bars

A sort of 'A' frame, fixed rigidly to the axle, and flexibly to the chassis. As the tyre is rotated by the axle, the axle, with its' ladder-bar extension, tries to rotate in the opposite direction. This rotation is transferred to the chassis as lift. The further forward the peak of the 'A' is mounted on the chassis, the further forward the point of lift, and the greater the leverage required to raise it. The top bar is under tension and the bottom in compression. The static alignment of the ladder-bar can be such that at rest some of that tension and compression, called pre-load, is already present.

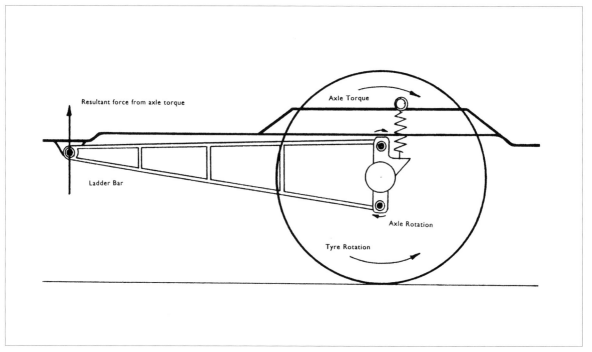

Ladder Bar.

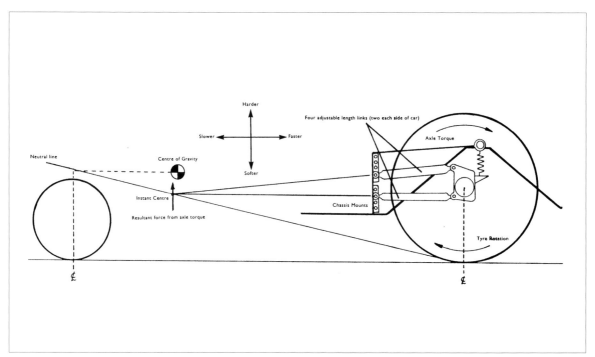

Four Link. The instant centre may be moved by adjustment of the 4-link lengths and their mounting points. The way the suspension reacts changes as the instant centre moves away from the neutral line. These changes are shown in the cruciform above, e.g. moving the instant centre above the neutral line causes the suspension to react harder and faster.

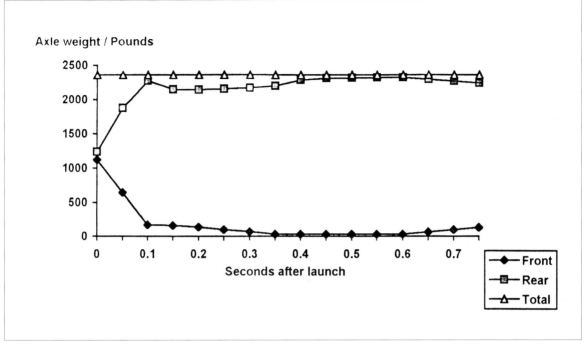

Dynamic Weight Transfer to rear wheels on launch with 4-link rear suspension, 2.5 G acceleration.

Four-link

Effectively a ladder-bar with the peak cut off. Attached to adjustable mountings, and with the top and bottom links of adjustable length, this is the most versatile form of drag racing suspension. This advantage is also its difficulty; with so many potential variables, the four-link is not easy to set up. Software is available that can predict the performance of a four-link set-up. It takes all the variables into account, including C of G position, shock rates, tyre size, wheelbase, etc. A wide variety of outputs are available, such as spring loading, shock forces and the like, but of significant interest here is tyre loading. The table shows overall car weight, alongside that for each of the front and rear axles, during the vital first second after launch. Notice how rapidly the front weight drops, and how the weight on the rear tyres is almost constant. After that vital first second, the inertia is overcome, and the nose can come down again to correct the aerodynamics.

Pre-Load

Pre-load has been mentioned above. Not only can this work by forcing the front up but, by dialling asymmetrical pre-load into the four-link set-up, the suspension can be adjusted to counteract the engine torque. That torque is trying to turn the car around its' longitudinal axis in the opposite direction to the engine rotation and dig one tyre in harder than the other. This would give an uneven grip which is undesirable, so the pre-load is set to even up the loads.

Not everyone has access to four-link. Chassis tuning is an art. Many crew chiefs have an instinctive grasp on the chassis setup and their experience is invaluable. It shows by their teams' consistency. One of the most experienced is probably Robinson Race Cars, who have built most of the cars competing in Pro Modified.

Andy Taylor. Honda CBX 1320 cc.

The Search For Power

A weather station used to measure the air density helps to predict the car's performance.

Armed with an idea of traction and suspension set-up and a reasonable engine, we want more power. Or do we want more torque? Torque is the amount of turning force an engine can produce. To move a heavy weight a lot of torque is needed. Acceleration from rest is provided by torque.

Power is work done; how much is moved how far, how soon. Our top speed will be determined by power, or how many torque strokes we can get out of our engine in the shortest time. A graph of power output plotted against rpm will show the power rise with increasing rpm, simply because we get more bangs into each minute.

For a bike, provided we have enough power to move it at high speed, less torque is used because there is a lower mass to move. Small, high revving bike engines are good for power, but lack torque. A car, being heavier, needs a lot of torque and power. Big, slow engines, like steam pumping engines have huge torque, but comparatively low power. For drag cars, there is no substitute for cubic inches. Big engines revving to their limit.

Power comes from burning fuel and the resultant expansion of gases. But additional fuel has to be balanced with additional oxygen, so that it has something with which to burn. There are various ways to get that extra oxygen in.

Air is drawn into the engine on the induction stroke, along with the fuel. As the rpm rises, so the amount of air that can be drawn in on each stroke changes. Factors like the exhaust rushing out, drawing some inlet air in behind it during valve overlap (that period when both valves are open), and tuned inlet manifolds, mean that there is a certain rpm when the airflow is best. That will be the rpm when the engine produces maximum torque. Above that figure, the power output will still rise, because we are getting strokes more often, but it will not rise so fast, because each stroke is now less torquey as the air cannot get in quick enough.

Eventually we reach one of two limits; either no more air can get in at all and, therefore, no more power is produced so the power curve flattens off, or the bits can't go round that fast anyway and something breaks. These are the art of the engine builder, tuning the engine to adjust the power and torque curves to best suit each application.

Turbo and Supercharging

These are the well-known means of boosting an engine. Use a fan to stuff in more air, so that extra fuel can be burned.

The Turbocharger uses the exhaust from the engine to drive the fan. A turbine in the exhaust drives a shaft, connected to an impeller in the inlet side, that may either suck or blow through the carburettor. The faster the exhaust goes, the more the turbo boosts, so it helps more at higher rpms. A valve called a waste-gate is fitted, to let excess pressure out of the inlet side — on gear changes for example. It is more common to find a turbo on bikes than cars in drag racing, because the cars want more torque. Compressing the air on the way in makes it hot and when the engine compresses it again the fuel may ignite before you want it to, called detonation. For this reason, turboed engines are usually run with a lower compression ratio, to delay the onset of detonation.

On the track, without silencers, the turbo bikes are noticeable because the turbo takes the bite out of the exhaust note. Except on the gear change, when the waste-gate pops open for a moment, frequently accompanied by a bang and flash of flame from the exhaust. The turbo is useful because the exhaust is `free' energy; only a small amount of power is lost driving the turbine. On the line, a turbo bike or car will be heard revving the engine to keep the revs up into the range where the turbo boost

Inside a supercharger

occurs. If, as the clutch is let in, the revs fall below the boost band, the driver has to wait for the revs to climb again before peak power is produced (called turbo lag). The racer will appear to bog down just off the line before surging off to try and catch his opponent.

The supercharger or blower, on the other hand, is driven from the crankshaft, usually by a toothed belt. It can often be seen under the carburettor or injector head, and be fitted directly to the inlet manifold. Pulley ratios can be varied to select the speed at which the supercharger turns in relation to the crank. Two helixes with nylon blades turn in opposite directions in a specially designed casting. Very nearly the same boost is available right across the rev range, so extra power and torque are available from idle to the rev limit.

However, the same detonation problem presents itself as with the turbo. And the inlet manifold is full of hot pressurised air and fuel. Significant safeguards are incorporated to control potential damage from an explosion in the inlet manifold. But, most importantly, the supercharger takes a lot of power itself. A 1,000hp engine might produce 2,000hp with a blower fitted, but it could take 500 extra horses to turn the blower pulley.

Both the turbo and supercharger are very good at adding extra power to an engine, but they are hardly the type of tuning aid that can be fitted by the novice racer. Each requires a large amount of work, expertise and expense to get right. Fitted to a Street car they affect Street driveability. If you need to commute in your racing car, something more flexible is needed.

Nitrous Oxide injection

So far we've added power by pushing more air into the engine, but most of the air is nitrogen (and other sundry gases). Only 24 per cent of air is oxygen by weight whereas nitrous oxide is 36 per cent oxygen — if we can get at it.

Nitrous oxide (N_2O), often wrongly abbreviated to NOS, is two atoms of nitrogen bonded to one of oxygen. It is colourless, non flammable, and smells slightly sweet. If inhaled a lot it will put you to sleep and if inhaled a little it will cause mild hysteria and bouts of giggling — hence its common name; laughing gas.

At around 300 degrees Celsius, the bonds between the atoms break and we have free nitrogen and oxygen to play with. If we squirt some N_2O (and a bit of extra fuel) into the engine instead of some air, when the piston rises on the compression stroke, the temperature rapidly rises, the N_2O releases extra oxygen and we've got extra power. If we squirt in a lot of N_2O and extra fuel, we get a lot of extra power. Naturally, the extra power is only wanted at full throttle, not in a public car park, so a microswitch on the carburettor linkage actuates solenoid operated valves for each of the N_2O and fuel injectors. A safety arming switch on the dashboard disables the whole system when not required.

Is N_2O the miracle additive that makes a Trabant launch like an F-18 fighter jet and do a five second pass? Not quite. The amount of N_2O and fuel injected at any time has to be carefully balanced. If the balance is wrong, the engine could burn a hole in a piston. Ratios and amounts are controlled by the size of the injector jets used. The engine must be able to take the added combustion pressures without blowing-up. The chassis and suspension set-up must be able to take the extra power; it is no use adding 500bhp on the line if all you're going to do is light-up the tyres.

N$_2$0 plumbing around a bike engine.

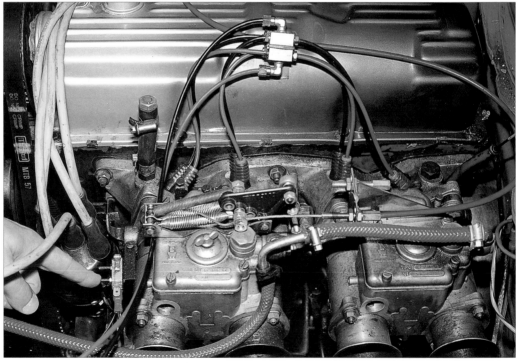

N$_2$0 plumbing around a car engine. The finger points to the full-throttle microswitch.

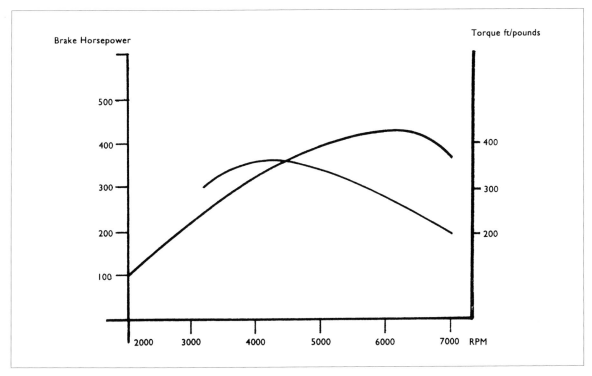

Brake Horsepower

Torque ft/pounds

500

400

300

200

100

400

300

200

2000   3000   4000   5000   6000   7000   RPM

A power vs torque curve.

A typical system for Street class use would use a delay box, to allow the car to get moving, and bring the N_2O in after perhaps a second. A more complex two stage system would perhaps add 50bhp on the launch, with another 100bhp two seconds later. Only with a very serious rear end set-up such as on a Pro Modified car, would a full multi-stage 500bhp system be of much use.

Nitrous can be combined with turbo or supercharging, such that the cold gas injected cools the hot air blown in, but this requires a specialist degree of cunning and is likely to be beyond the scope of most people.

Nitrous Oxide injection does present an easy-to-fit, reasonably priced route to tuning, especially in the Street classes. (Make sure it's legal in that class though!) Class sponsors for both the Euro Series and the Rover Challenge are heavily involved with Nitrous Oxide systems for that very reason. Spray-bar systems, where the Nitrous and fuel are injected from a plate fitted between the carburettor and the manifold are the most simple to fit, being a straightforward job for most mechanics.

A system with multi-fogger nozzles that mix the fuel and nitrous at the point of injection and inject it immediately into each inlet port, will give harder hitting results, but will need a partial engine strip. It is recommended that the seriously curious contact one of the class sponsors for details. A class with the word 'stock' in the title means that Nitrous is expressly forbidden, for example, Pro-stock bike.

Purging the Nitrous

On a hard-hitting system, the N_2O injected should be liquid, not gas. Stored under pressure on a cylinder away from the engine, it is piped to the solenoid valves near the inlet manifold, and then to the injectors. These pipes warm up near the engine,

Top: Nitrous Oxide injection.

Left: a plate injection for placing between the comb and the manifold.

Centre: an NOS bottle and it's mountings together with the solenoids and associated wiring.

Right: fogger nozzles for fitting into the inlet manifold — one for each inlet port.

vapourising the gas inside. Just before a run, an extra solenoid valve is manually actuated, venting the nitrous where the driver can see it, so that he can ensure that the whole system is primed with liquid. On a Street car, the vapourised nitrous injected first, followed by the liquid, will make for a more progressive, softer hitting effect.

Aerodynamics

Any object that is expected to cut through the air at close to 300mph has got to consider aerodynamics.

Jens Nybo. On two wheels at the Hockenheim $^{1}/_{8}$th mile mark, August 1995.

Copyright: Martin Grosse Geldermann

Any object that is expected to cut through the air at pushing 300mph has got to consider aerodynamics. It works for you and against you. The against is fairly obvious. The for is that at speeds over about 100mph, the rear wing surface can generate a large amount of downforce. This force, operating behind the rear axle to use leverage to advantage, pushes the rear wheels hard into the track, enabling the clutch to come in harder and sooner. The front of the car needs to be forced into the track to counterbalance both the rear wing and the torque reaction of the rear wheels.

Watching a dragster at speed, you'll notice that the chassis bows in the middle; the wheels and wing are trying to lift the front, and the front wing (canard) is trying to push it back down.

The picture of 1995 ETFA Champion Jens Nybo at speed, above, demonstrates many of these effects. He kept telling his crew that he was picking up the front end a bit at half track; here's proof.

The downforce from the rear wing can be seen by the distortion of the rear tyre. The top of the tyre has narrowed because of the speed, the rear edge has straightened as the wheels pull the rubber rapidly round to the front, stretching the back edge, and the tyre is splayed out at the track surface, a reaction to the downforce. This downforce has also lifted the front slightly (although here exaggerated because there is a slight bump in the Hockenheim track as it goes over the tunnel to the centre area.)

It is desirable for the launch of a Top Fuel dragster to lift the front wheels for the first one hundred feet or so, as it maximises weight transfer to the rear. Problems arise if the front of the car rises enough to put the front wings (Canard wings) into negative camber. These are normally angled down about six degrees to keep the front down at speed and when the rear wing is applying some 3000 kilos of force behind the rear axle, the canards need to provide around 800 kilos to counterbalance it. If at any time, the front rises more than six degrees, the canards will be providing lift and a blowover invariably results. The early blowovers in the USA occurred at the top of the track when some part of the equation went wrong. Because of the inertia within the tyres and transmission simply coming off, the power will not slow the car down quick enough.

This picture sequence was taken by cool amateur photographer, John Burleton, from the spectator bank. The driver, Rico Anthes, equally coolly, waited for the car to come to rest, went through his normal shutdown sequence, climbed out of his car unhurt and bowed to the applauding crowd!

Funny Car Aerodynamics

With their shorter wheelbase, Funny cars do not have the inherent missile like stability of Dragsters, nor do they have the same degree of weight transfer available. They have a greater frontal area, so have a greater area to push through the air. For these reasons they are slightly slower than the long cars. But their shape is more efficient; the whole body acts to keep the airflow smooth. The rear wing (that must not be separate from the bodywork) creates a large downforce onto the rear wheels. Because the airflow over the car is smoother, there is less need for it to be raised. The amount of turbulent air created behind the wing by the downforce above it, can be seen by the cloud of clutch dust that follows one of these things away from the line.

Top Fuel

The power output is so huge that the idea is to run the engine within an inch of its life for four-and-a-half to five seconds and then shut it off quickly before it blows up.

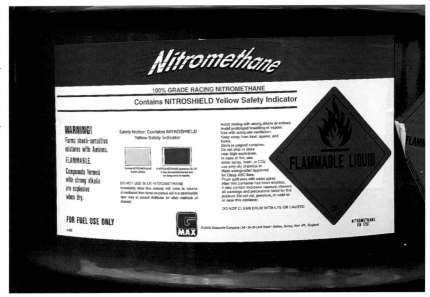

Top Fuel engines are developed from the Chrysler 426 ci Big Block Hemi so, in effect, are a relatively low technology pushrod V8.* They do not have multi-overhead cams or multi-valves. They're not allowed sophisticated electronic engine management systems or ignitions. It is important that the engine is capable of being quickly dismantled and easily rebuilt. The power output is so huge that the idea is to run it within an inch of its' life for four-and-a-half to five seconds and then shut it off quickly, just before it blows up. You then take it all apart, replace the broken bits like worn bearing shells, burnt pistons, etc. Put it back together and, an hour later, try not to blow it up again. (*The Australian McGee brothers have developed an overhead cam, four valve per cylinder Top Fuel engine, but it is still a rare beast. We are unaware of any in use in Europe).

So what is the secret of getting 5,000hp out of an engine designed for 500hp? How do you get it onto the track if you don't have a gearbox? Since power comes from burning fuel and oxygen together, you blow vast amounts of a special kind of fuel (that contains lots of its own oxygen) into the cylinder using a supercharger. Squeeze the air you blew it in with until it all gets good and hot, hit the mixture with a really big spark and retire to a safe distance. To leave the line quickly, slip the clutch progressively less for the first two-and-a-half seconds or so and finally lock it solid until you get to the end of the quarter mile. A big wing helps. Come off the loud pedal, put in the clutch, switch off the fuel, coast to a stop and wait for your crew to tow you back to the pits. It's dead easy.

Nitromethane

The crucial ingredient to Top Fuel racing is the fuel itself. Whereas an eight-litre gasoline engine can develop around 800hp and a supercharged-alcohol engine around 2,000hp, the limit comes when it is no longer possible to push more air and fuel into the engine. Gasoline needs around one part fuel to 15.5 parts air to burn efficiently. Methanol needs around one part fuel to six parts air. With more than twice the amount of fuel available, even though it's not quite as efficient a fuel (less power per unit volume) more power is produced. Both of these fuels burn with the oxygen. A part of the fuel/air mixture is ignited by the spark and a flame-front travels through the mixture, burning as it goes. They are a low explosive.

In contrast Nitromethane, which is a name for a type of Nitric-acid-enriched propane, does not actually burn. Drop a match in it and the match goes out. But under conditions of extreme pressure and temperature it will explode. The difference is that when the spark arrives and ignites a bit of the mixture, the reaction-front moves with the speed of the shockwave through the mixture, far faster than a flame and irrespective of the presence of oxygen. When hot and under pressure Nitro is a high explosive.

The air is forced into the engine by the supercharger and a certain amount of the fuel is sprayed in with it. More fuel is added at high pressure directly into the inlet manifold and yet more immediately behind the inlet valve, until the fuel/air ratio is around 2.5:1. As the piston comes up on the compression stroke, the temperature of the air rises dramatically and heats the fuel until the conditions are right for the spark; the air is only required because liquids do not compress. Top Fuel engines need to use magnetos to generate the ignition, because magnetos develop a much longer and more powerful spark. In fact they use two of them, feeding one spark-plug per cylinder each. This is because there is so much fuel going into a modern Top Fuel engine that it could swamp a single spark.

The fuel is pumped constantly, on all four strokes of the cycle. Timed injection systems were outlawed to keep costs down, along with engine management computers. The fuel pressure is around 200psi, and the flow rate is enormous; around two thirds of a

A maze of fuel lines weave between the valves on the head.

The blower is lifted onto the engine.

The two Magnetos are clearly visible as is their size.

The unburned fuel streams out of a dropped cylinder.

gallon per second. If a particular cylinder does not fire, the unburnt fuel comes out of the exhaust headers in a thick white jet. Problems occur — slight understatement — if it doesn't all come out, for instance if an exhaust valve stem breaks. When more fuel is poured in on the next cycle, the piston comes up and, well, remember the bit about a liquid not compressing? The phenomenon is known in Top Fuel as Hydraulicking; something has to give and it's not gonna be the fuel. If you're lucky a con rod breaks and comes out the side of the block. It is referred to as windowing the block and can usually be welded up again. If you're less lucky the whole engine comes apart at the seams. Either way, it's frighteningly spectacular when it happens, but the diapers and blankets and so on are designed to any flying bits.

Of course, it might have been an inlet valve that has stuck open. The difficulty here is that the Supercharger is merrily cramming more fuel and air into the inlet manifold and sooner or later the cylinder with the stuck valve is going to spark. Before steps were taken to limit the effect of this, superchargers were launched hundreds of feet by the resultant explosion. Nowadays the inlet manifold has a built-in weak spot called a burst plate and the blower has thick fireproof webbing belts to restrain it if there is a bang big enough to go for launch.

The power the engine produces is adjusted by varying the exact ratio of Nitro and Methanol from 100 per cent Nitro (quite rare) down to around 92 per cent Nitro (or sometimes down to 50 per cent for exhibition cars). In the region of 97 per cent is most common.

The supercharger drive-ratio can be changed by changing the top pulley size. These would be altered by the crew chief and are determined by air temperature, humidity and pressure. The other factor he will consider is the track condition; with cool, dense air he will get best power from the engine, but the track has to be sticky enough to take it. All he has to do is get it onto the track.

The multi-plate clutch clearances being measured and set before a run.

After a run the clutch may have worn by 70 thousandths of an inch, be covered in dust and too hot to touch for at least an hour.

Copyright: Crispin Driver

A block, not so much windowed as 'patio-doored'.

The Clutch

Paradoxically, it is the clutch that is the centre of the crew chief's attention. Assuming he has a reliable engine and has set the fuel and blower ratios for the maximum power given the weather conditions, the clutch is the primary tuning component at his disposal. Whereas very early fuellers would let the clutch out quickly and spin the tyres for most of the track, later ones slipped the clutch for the first part of the track and put in lower times. Until the late eighties two-speed Lenco transmissions, similar to those used by Top Alcohol cars today, were still being used. The clutch locks up in around half-a-second and then the driver hits a steering-wheel-mounted shift button for the higher gear.

Around 1990, the direct drive system with slider clutch was the way to go. A centrifugal clutch works by a system of weighted levers. When the engine revs rise, as the throttle is opened, the weights are thrown outward by centrifugal force and the levers press the clutch together, gripping the driven plates. Note that a Top Fuel engine will rev from idle to 7,000rpm in around 0.1 seconds. On a slider clutch, the sliding limiting mechanism initially only lets a few levers operate and then, as it moves, progressively more levers come into play. So the clutch will initially grip gently and slip a lot, and gradually slip less and grip more, until it grips solid. There are no gears.

The amount of grip at each stage can be controlled by adjusting the weight on the levers (actually no more than a combination of nuts and washers). The speed of the slider is controlled by compressed air. Remember, electronic control is not allowed. So, a pneumatic timer, started when the accelerator pedal is floored, releases compressed air in a series of stages through a series of escape valves, which control the movement of the slider. That is why during a run, although the car may leave the line cleanly (albeit in a cloud of black clutch dust), the tyres may spin some distance down the

A multi-stage pneumatic timer controls both the clutch and the fuel system.

track (lighting up the tyres). This is either because that stage of clutch came in too quickly, or it gripped too much. If the driver is experienced, and quick enough, he may back-off the power for an instant but the race may already have been won in the other lane. For the next run, the crew chief would either reduce the weights a little, or lengthen the delay with the pneumatic timers; called taking out some clutch. The objective of course is to lock-up the clutch as soon as possible without lighting up the tyres. But the engine and clutch is all set up in the pits by the crew; if all goes well it is the driver's job just to react to the green light and steer the beast.

Fuellers at night are an awesome sight. When we took this half second exposure shot we expected to see a continuous streak of flame. Instead, every exhaust pulse is visible.

After a Top Alcohol engine has eaten its innards, any means can be used to raise the funds for a re-build.

Classes and Timing

Racing is against the guy in the other lane, qualifying is against the clock.

Pete Ashworth's Ford Pop suffers a nitrous burp.

There are three types of drag race with subtle differences:- Class, Index and Bracket racing. Both Class and Index are Professional races, whereas Bracket, also known as the Sportsmen class, is where racers run cars to suit their budget.

Class racing

In Class racing, the cars and bikes are relatively evenly matched, and also meet the class requirements. This is Heads-Up racing; two vehicles leave the start together and the first to the finish line wins — no handicap timing system is used. The start lights are set to a Pro Tree — with all three ambers on together and the green following 0.4 of a second later. These classes are Top Fuel Dragster, Funny Car, Top Alcohol, Pro Modified, Top Fuel Bike, Funny Bike, Pro Stock Bike, Competition Bike, Outlaw Anglia, Pro Rover, Pro Euro and some VW's.

Index racing

Index racing is similar, except that the Class has an Index limit; 'Thou shalt not run faster than thine Index, or thou art disqualified.' For example, 10.90 Bikes must not go under 10.90 seconds. This would be termed breaking-out. It is still the first driver to reach the finish line who wins, unless both break-out, in that case whoever breaks out the least will win. These classes are Super Gas (9.90 breakout), 9.90 Bike, 10.90 bike, and Street Rover (11.00 breakout).

Bracket racing

In Bracket (also known as ET) racing, a handicap system is used with the start lights set to a *Sportsman Tree*. Here each of the three amber lights are lit in turn, half-a-second apart, the green following another half-a-second after the third amber. Competitors run within a particular *Elapsed-Time* bracket which they feel to be competitive, but with the handicap start to make for very close racing at the top end of the track. So an 11 second car might race against a 13 second car, although the latter would get the green light first. The objective is still to be the first to the finish line without going under your predicted ET.

Dialling-in

ET's are predicted for Bracket racing. If during practice a driver achieves times of 11.52, 11.53 and 11.55 seconds, he could set his predicted lowest ET of 11.50 seconds, or a Dial-in of 11.50. He knows that if he goes flat out, he will take just over 11.50 seconds for his run. He writes his Dial-in onto the rear window of his car with shoe whitener, so that it can be clearly read by the timekeeper.

His competitor in the other lane might set his Dial-in at 13.00 seconds. As both cars approach the start line, the timekeeper will enter each of the Dial-ins into the timing computer, which will work out the handicap required; in this case 1.50 seconds. When the starter presses the go button, the Christmas Tree will start the count-down for the slower car immediately and one-and-a-half seconds later than for the faster car.

As with all racing it is still the first driver to reach the finish line who will win, unless both break-out, in that case whoever breaks-out the least wins. The classes are Super Pro ET; 7.00 to 8.48, Pro ET; 8.49 to 9.99, Modified ET; 10.00 to 11.49, Super ET; 11.50 to 13.49, Street ET; 13.49 and slower, and Street Euro.

In general we will refer to National Competition throughout this book. For regional events, the entrants maybe split into Pro (faster than say 12 seconds) and Sportsman (slower then Pro.) This is the system used at Avon Park Shootouts, for example. Other tracks and events may use different break times. The competitors are numbered simply P or S followed by their race number.

The Pre-Stage & Stage beams & detectors by the front wheels of Steve Dunn's Tokyo Toy Toyota Celica.

Reaction time

The common feature about all of the above racing classifications is the objective of getting both cars together to the finish line. So where is the competition? The answer is on the line. The clock that measures the ET is not started by the green light, as is commonly believed, but by the front wheels leaving the stage beam. If two cars run 10.00 exactly, on a 9.90 index, but one takes one second to react to the lights, he will lose by that one second.

The drivers' reaction-time (RT) is measured from the time the last amber light comes on (or all of them on a Pro Tree), until the ET clock is started by the front wheels leaving the stage beam. Thus a perfect Sportsman reaction time is 0.5 seconds, and 0.4 seconds for Pro. If one driver has a quicker RT than the other, the difference is known as a Hole Shot and the slower driver is playing chase; he may not be able to catch up without breaking-out!

The ultimate object is to start just as the green light comes on, not before and not after. If a driver leaves before the green light, detected by an RT less than the perfect 0.4 or 0.5, the timing devices will light the red foul light instead of the green. This may be called by the nickname of leaving a cherry on the tree, or red-lighting

Qualifying

Usually at a drag race event, all competitors have to qualify before the true racing starts. This is especially so when there are perhaps 14 competitors and only space in the event timetable for eight to race. All 14 cars would get a chance to run against the clock but only the fastest eight will get through to establish an eight car field. Qualifying may occur one vehicle at a time, but more usually in pairs; although side-by-side qualifying does look like a race. In the 14 to eight car example, the time for the eighth place car is known as the bump-spot. In a further round of qualifying, if you can run

The Christmas Tree

Pro-Tree

The left-hand lane is in Pre-Stage. The blue light indicates that the timing computer is ready – the cars are not called forward into stage until the blue light is lit.

Both lanes are in Pre-Stage.

The right-hand lane is in Full-Stage. The left-hand lane is still waiting in Pre-Stage.

Both lanes are in Full-Stage. The starter will now trip the tree. Up to this point, Pro-tree and Sportsman are the same.

The ambers all appear together for 0.4 seconds.

Provided both cars are still in Full-Stage, the green appears. If one is not, his/her lane will get a red light.

Sportsman-Tree

Both cars are in Pre-Stage. If the two cars are running different dial-ins, these will have been loaded into the computer. In this example we are going to give the right-hand lane an advantage.

The starter runs the tree and the right-hand lane starts to count down in 0.5 second intervals.

T + 0.5 seconds. The right-hand lane is counting down 0.5 seconds ahead of the left. But the right-hand driver has crept forward out of Pre-Stage into Deep-Stage. He/She is dangerously close to red lighting.

T + one second. Countdown continues.

T + one-and-a-half seconds. The left-hand lane is about to get the green. The right-hand lane rolled out of stage before the green appeared and hence gets a red light.

T + two seconds. The left-hand lane has a green light and goes. The right-hand lane is disqualified if it is in an eliminations round, but posts the lowest qualifying time if it is in a qualifying race.

56

The burnout box is a shallow depression with enough water in it to wet the tyres. Timing beams each have lamps or sensors on the centre line — popular targets for competitors who get out of shape on a run. No crew may touch a car or bike after it has reached the hands-off line.

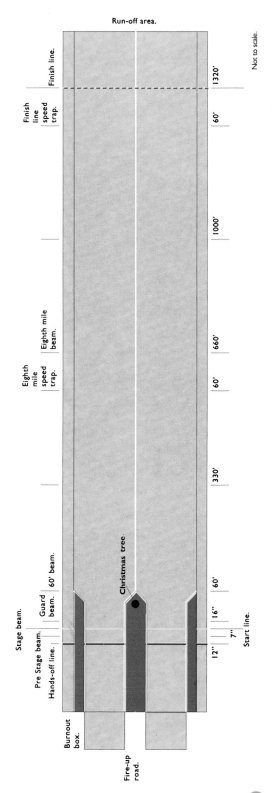

Run-off area.

Finish line.

Not to scale.

Finish line speed trap.

Eighth mile speed trap.

Eighth mile beam.

Stage beam.

Pre Stage beam. Hands-off line.

Guard beam.

60' beam.

Christmas tree.

Burnout box.

Fire-up road.

Start line.

1320'

60'

1000'

660'

60'

330'

60'

16"

7"

12"

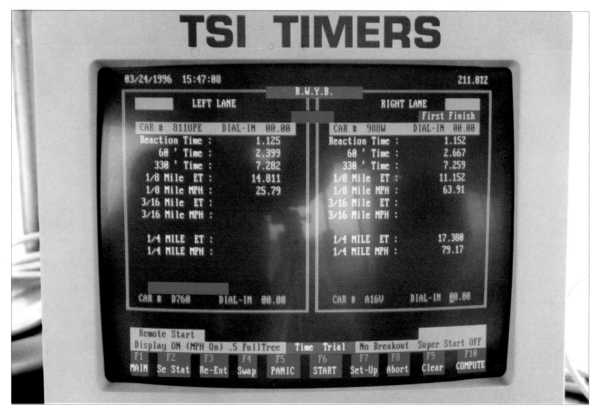

TSI TIMERS

03/24/1996 15:47:00				211.012

R.W.Y.B.

LEFT LANE		RIGHT LANE	
			First Finish
CAR # 811UPE DIAL-IN 00.00		CAR # 988W DIAL-IN 00.00	
Reaction Time :	1.125	Reaction Time :	1.152
60 ' Time :	2.399	60 ' Time :	2.667
330 ' Time :	7.202	330 ' Time :	7.259
1/8 Mile ET :	14.811	1/8 Mile ET :	11.152
1/8 Mile MPH :	25.79	1/8 Mile MPH :	63.91
3/16 Mile ET :		3/16 Mile ET :	
3/16 Mile MPH :		3/16 Mile MPH :	
1/4 MILE ET :		1/4 MILE ET :	17.380
1/4 MILE MPH :		1/4 MILE MPH :	79.17
CAR # D760 DIAL-IN 00.00		CAR # A16U DIAL-IN 00.00	

Remote Start
Display ON (MPH On) .5 FullTree   Time Trial   No Breakout   Super Start OFF

F1	F2	F3	F4	F5	F6	F7	F8	F9	F10
MAIN	Se Stat	Re-Ent	Swap	PANIC	START	Set-Up	Abort	Clear	COMPUTE

faster than the Bump-Spot, then you take a place in the qualified field and the eighth place holder gets bumped. The finish line timing boards will indicate the bump-spot time during qualifying so that the competitors and crowd can see the target to be beaten.

Additionally, in qualifying, the timing boards will display the reaction times during each run with these being replaced by the terminal speed as the car goes through the finish line speed-trap. A red light does not count in qualifying, only in racing, and the displayed RT is useful for the driver to set up his launch routine for the particular track conditions. Class indexes do count however, and a driver unlucky enough to run under his index goes to the bottom of the qualifying list; if another goes under, the one nearest to the index moves up the list.

This is the Timer screen as seen by the Timekeeper. The Interval times are shown, except that the car in the left-hand lane broke and is marooned beyond the half-track point.

Class Name	Abbreviation	Handicap	Heads Up	Sports Start	Pro Start	Index	Tread Tyres	Slick Tyres	Wheelie Bars	Pump Petrol	Racing Petrol	Nitrous Oxide	Turbo	Supercharger	Weight Breaks	Methanol	Nitromethane
Sportsman Street Elim.	SSE		*	*			*			*		*	*	*			
Pro Street Eliminator	PSE		*		*			*			*						
VW Street	VW S	*		*		>14.99	*			*		*	*	*			
VW Super Street	VW SS	*		*		Dial		*	*	*	*	*	*	*			
VW Kits and Specials	VW KS	*		*		>11.99		*	*	*	*	*	*	*		*	*
VW Modified	VW M		*	*		<11.99		*	*	*	*	*	*	*		*	*
Street Euro	ES	*		*		Dial		*		*	*	*	*	*			
Pro Euro	EP	*	*					*		*	*	*	*	*			
Street ET	St ET	*		*		13.49	*	*		*		*	*	*			
Super ET	Su ET	*		*		11.50	*	*		*	*	*	*	*			
Modified ET	Mod ET	*		*		10.00	*	*		*	*	*	*	*		*	
Pro ET	Pro ET	*		*		8.49		*		*	*	*	*	*		*	*
Super Pro ET	SP ET	*		*		7.00		*		*	*	*	*	*		*	*
Sportsman Bike	SP		*		*	10.90	*			*		*	*	*			
Street Bike	SB		*		*	9.90	*			*		*	*	*			
Super Street Bike	SS		*		*		*			*		*	*	*			
Supertwin Street	STS		*	*			*			*							
Supertwin Modified	STM		*	*				*		*	*	*or	*or	*			
Supertwin Top Gas	STG		*	*				*		*	*						
Supertwin Top Fuel	STF		*	*				*					*	*		*	*
Pro Stock Bike	PS		*	*				*	*	*	*				*		
Competition Bike	CB		*	*				*	*	*	*	*	*	*		*	*
Funny Bike	FB		*	*				*	*	*	*	*	*	*		*	*
Top Fuel Bike	TF		*	*				*	*				*	*		*	*
Street Rover	SR		*	*		11.00	*			*	*	*or	*or	*			
Super Street Rover	SSR		*	*				*	*	*	*	*	*	*			
Pro Rover	PR		*	*				*	*	*	*	*	*	*			
Wild Bunch	W		*	*		Dial		*	*	*	*	*	*	*	*	*	*
Outlaw Anglia	OA		*	*				*	*	*	*	*	*	*		*	*
Super Gas	SG		*	*		9.90		*	*	*	*	*	*	*		*	
Super Competiton	SC		*	*		8.90		*	*	*	*	*	*	*		*	
Pro Modified	Pro		*	*				*	*	*	*	*	*	*	*	*	
Top Alcohol Funny Car	TA/FC		*	*				*	*				*	*	*	*	
Top Alcohol Dragster	TA/D		*	*				*	*				*	*	*	*	
Funny Car	AA/FC		*	*				*	*					*			*
Top Fuel Dragster	TF		*	*				*	*					*			*

A table comparing some of the main features of each class. The Sportsman Street Eliminator, Pro Street Eliminator (were one class) and Super Street Rover and Super Comp. are classes that started in 1996 and hence are not covered in the following pages. The * denotes a features that may be used, or is mandatory, in that class.

RWYB/ Test 'n' Tune/ Gary's Picnic/ Mopar Nationals

One of the highlights of the weekend is the Burnout Competition. Who can do the biggest and best? It is utterly pointless, totally mindless, absolutely insane and irresistible fun, which leaves all who witness it wearing a huge, stupid grin.

Drag racing, for most new entrants, starts at Run what you Brung or Test 'n' Tune. These races are the same, but they have different names and are held in different places. This is where skills in reaction time and record keeping can be developed. Each run should be documented from the outset, noting weather conditions, car set-up and the results. Later on, as changes are made, it becomes easier to determine the effect of those changes. In a further racing career, it gives the competitor a database of set-up information to suit each track condition. All three permanent venues will work together from 1996, to develop the RWYB format. A new low cost National Street Racer Championship will be jointly promoted, to bring cheap competitive drag racing to a wider field.

Gary's Picnic

Gary's picnic is an annual event run by the BDRA. They have a fully portable timing set-up including tree, lights and quarter mile cables. With that they can work anywhere. This event was held at the North Weald airfield, just north of London. It is not actually a race event, but one where pairs of cars or bikes do side-by-side test runs, just like in RWYB.

Mopar Nationals

Mopar is the motorsport arm of the Chrysler corporation. Annually there is an event where only Mopar powered cars compete, usually at Santa Pod. Held over a weekend, it is slightly more formal than an event like Gary's Picnic, in as much as there is real racing. To be a real race an event needs to be RAC sanctioned, with RAC observers present. This costs more to put on than a non race event. There are still display areas and speed parts stalls, etc. Many of the regular ET Mopars come out for an opportunity of doing some heads-up racing. Awards include Fastest Mopar, King of the Street (the winner of the eliminations), Show 'n' Go, Burnout Competition, etc. Other events include Fast Ford, and the ubiquitous VW raves (see elsewhere). But most racing in the UK is within the IHRA UK National Championship, under the formal authorisation of the RACMSA/ACU.

Burnout Competition.

Gary's Picnic.

Street Eliminator (SE)

A 'streetable' car is one that you could drive to the shops for the Friday evening rush hour when it rains.

The general principle behind this custom car class is to find the fastest street car in Britain. Crucial to this, is the subtle difference between a car that is 'Street Legal' and one that is 'Streetable' — the latter you could drive to the shops for the Friday evening rush hour when it rains. The former might have lights and an MOT, but only a half gallon tank, no alternator, and a cooling system that the King's Road would boil in under a minute! They need not apply. The racing occurs in three stages. Qualifying on the Saturday of an event will be on a heads-up basis, to give an eight car field and four alternates (with demand this may change in future seasons to 16 + 4). These cars will then be required to complete a 12-25 mile observed cruise, on public roads, on the Saturday night. This will include a fuel stop where all competitors will be obliged to fill up with regular pump gas. They will have to prove their car capable of hot starting,

both at the fuel stop and the cruise destination. Jump or bump starting is not allowed, neither are spare batteries. Failure to hot start within two minutes will lead to disqualification from that round of the elimination. No chase/support vehicles will be allowed and the competitors must complete the cruise within 15 minutes of the pace vehicle. All vehicles must be fitted with a passenger seat mounted alongside the drivers' seat. For the elimination races slick tyres and open exhaust headers may be used. In the true tradition of no-holds-barred Outlaw street racing, Nitrous Oxide is positively encouraged. Drivers must wear a minimum single layer fire suit and RAC approved helmet. Cars should be prepared for the safety requirements appropriate to their times; for example mid 12's should meet Su ET rules and sub 10's Super Gas rules. From 1996 there will be Street and Pro Street.

Ian Kenyon. '64 Chrysler Vallant. 440 ci Mopar.

Alistair Cromie. Ford Anglia. 355 ci Chevy.

Gary Keep. '34 Ford 3 Window Coupe. 440 ci Chrysler.

Brian Arliss. '32 Ford Coupe. 406 ci Chevy.

Derek Annable. Nicknamed 'Grandad' by the Santa Pod commentators — he first started racing in 1994 at the ripe old age of 65!

Just one of the many vehicles which turn out regularly for RWYB but choose not to enter the competition. This Fiat is nudging 12 second passes at 120mph.

Street ET (ST ET)

>13.49 Seconds.

This was the natural starting point for aspiring racers who were impressed by their prowess at RWYB and wanted to get into real racing.

This was the natural starting point for aspiring racers who were impressed by their prowess at RWYB and wanted to get into real racing. With the addition of newer classes, like the Euro Challenge, this distinction is now becoming blurred. It is open to cars produced by a recognised manufacturer. The body must be of original length, with a minimum wheelbase of 90 inches and road legal mudguards over wheels. Any transmission is acceptable but it must be in the stock location as must the driver's seat. Additional frame members are permitted and four wheel brakes, and functional lights are also required. Nitrous oxide and slick tyres may be used, but only petrol fuel. A minimum single layer fire suit is required. Confusion amongst spectators is common, as the Street classes (Euro, Rover and Street Eliminator) freely and frequently intermingle if their regular class is not represented at a particular event. There is nothing illegal in this, provided the class restrictions are met — but naturally championship points cannot be carried from one class to another. Some modifications, specific for drag race use, appear in this class, with most entrants using line locks. Traction bar, ladder bar or four link rear end modifications are common for increased traction and weight transfer on launch.

Steve Harrington. Pontiac GTO. 400 ci Pontiac.

Paul Hudson. Ford Capri MK3. 2800 cc Ford — Lost Cause.

Ian Turnbull. Chevrolet Camaro SS. 396 ci Chevy — Plough II.

Mark Allen. 1968 Dodge Coronet. 360 ci Chrysler — Sub Lime.

Super ET (SU ET)

11.50-13.49 Seconds.

Surprisingly, most Drag racers use automatic transmissions. They change faster than a manual box and can be modified for manual control of automatic shifting.

Things start to get serious here. Having 'Done the Knowledge' of Street ET, lightened the body a bit, tweaked the suspension and so on, the car regularly breaks-out of 13.49, and you move up to Super ET. Bodies must retain stock axle location, with a minimum 90 inch wheelbase, may be chopped or streamlined, but must retain road legal mudguards — these may be fibreglass replicas of factory originals. Full bodied cars must retain two operating doors and handles for exit either side. Tube frame chassis are allowed. One tail light is required, but generator, fans, horn, wipers etc may be removed. If the headlights are removed they must be replaced with metal plates. Windows may be replaced with plexiglass which must have a minimum thickness of 1/8 inches. Side windows need not be openable but, if they are, they must be closed during competition. Only petrol is allowed — which may be racing fuel. A minimum single layer fire suit is required. Surprisingly, most drag racers use automatic transmissions. They change faster than a manual box and can be modified for manual control of automatic shifting. Gear changes can occur quickly at the rev-points selected by the driver. Amongst the benefits of this arrangement are greater consistency. It also gives the opportunity to link gear shift control with Nitrous oxide injection but, more importantly, an auto box can be fitted with a Trans Brake; a launch switch.

Trans Brake

This is a switch-controlled valve within an automatic gearbox that simultaneously selects both first and reverse gears. Thus as power is applied, the box sees equal pressure on both gears, locks up and goes nowhere. As the switch is released so reverse is released and the first gear, being already engaged, takes up immediately. The driver would move up to pre stage. When both cars are in pre stage and the driver is ready, he moves into full stage, stops with the brake, engages the trans brake and floors the throttle. The engine will only rev as far as the stall speed of the torque converter, as its output is locked by the gearbox (around 3-4000 rpm). To launch, the driver simply takes his finger off the trans brake button and the car launches hard as if the clutch had

Dave Day. 1932 Ford 3 Window Coupe. 460 ci — Days of Thunder.

just been dropped. There is more to it than that though. With practice the driver can determine exactly how long it takes for him to react to the light, how long for the trans brake valve to release, how long for the transmission and tyres to react and how long for the car to move from the start line. After the last yellow light, he then knows exactly when to release the button, in order to launch exactly with the green light — known as cutting a good light.

Torque Conversion

Instead of a clutch, an automatic box uses a torque converter. Where the difference in speed between the engine and gearbox is great, such as off the line, the converter will slip like a clutch. As the car speed increases, it progressively locks-up. Even better, is the torque magnification effect as the converter slips. That is why auto boxes usually have less gears than manuals. This is handy for drag racing. When the green light shows, the driver stamps on the gas. The torque converter slips, allowing the engine to rev into the power band without smoking the tyres. As the car gathers speed, the converter locks-up. When the gear change happens, be it auto or manual, the converter slips again, keeping the engine revs up. That is why the noise from a racing car doesn't often vary in note during a run; the revs may fluctuate by less than 1000 rpm from launch, through the gearchange to the finish line.

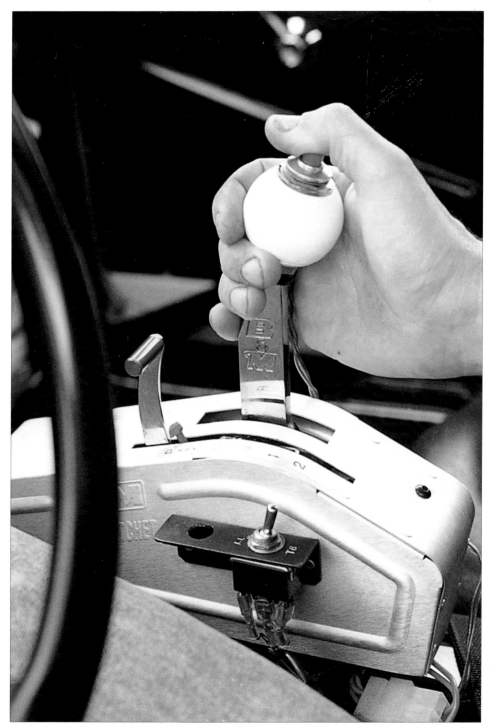

This driver has his thumb on the trans brake button on the top of his manually controlled auto gearbox shifter.
The switch on the side selects button action between trans brake and line lock.

Volkswagon Drag Racing Club (VWDRC)

Specialist Volkswagon weekends are very well supported and are one big party.

Volkswagon racing is not strictly within the mainstream of drag racing, in as much as dubbers rarely compete against anything but other Volkswagons. But they do have their own very dedicated following. Specialist Volkswagon event weekends are very well supported, with Volkswagon racing, Show 'n' Shine, auctions, discos, live music, funfairs etc, and are one big party. There are frequently guest classes invited, such as the Outlaw Anglias, or occasionally even Top Alcohol. There are currently four classes of Volkswagon racing. These are Street (VWS), Super Street (VWSS), Kits and Specials (VWKS) and Modified (VWM).

Scott Cutler. VW Street.

Jules Kennon. Kharman Ghia in Super Street.

Nathan Underwood. Crazy Days Kit Special.

'Bad' Bernie Smith. VW Modified Dragster.

Outrage III, driven by Paul Hughes, is a full nitro burning VW funny car. It always draws a crowd.

Street Bike

The Regulations for 10.90 bike (SP), 9.90 bike (SB) and Super Street bike (SS) are all very similar. The classes are open to bikes with a single engine. They may be of any type and any modification with unlimited cubic capacity. The frame must be based on a generally available road-going frame, but the steering-head geometry, trail and wheelbase may be altered to improve stability. The maximum permitted wheelbase is 1730mm, measured with the rear wheel at the most extended position allowed by the swing-arm. Nitrous oxide injection, Superchargers and Turbochargers of any type or pattern are allowed as long as the fuel used is petrol only. Wheels may be of any type and size that complies with the Road Traffic Act. Tyres must be readily available street tyres with a minimum of 2mm of tread depth. Wheelie-bars are not permitted. Suspension must be original factory equipment. Pattern-type shock absorbers are allowed and rear struts may be used.

Tony Clark. Suzuki GSXR1100. 1500 cc.

Pete Marshall. Harris Kawasaki. 1260 cc.

Andy Tysziewicz. Suzuki EF. 1260 cc.

Karl Larcombe. Suzuki Katana. 1170 cc.

Chris Hannam. Suzuki GSXTurbo. 1398 cc.

Euro Challenge

The Euro Challenge is intended as an alternative to those classes filled with huge hunks of Detroit iron. It grew out of the now defunct Four-Pot Challenge. Led by Highpower Nitrous Systems' Trevor Langfield. Not unsurprisingly it aims to prove that a decent European four-pot with properly set up Nitrous Oxide Injection can run reasonable ET's. Vince Bunn of Catchit Cars shares this aim, hoping to use a Cosworth Turbo with gas to run regularly in the nines. It is open to any European car produced by a recognised European manufacturer. Any engine of any size made for the European market is permitted, with any form of tuning and modification. An American V8 fitted as original equipment to a British car is only permitted in the original body shell. Although cars should appear to be street legal, with fully working suspension and lights, any tyres are allowed. Racing is on a dial-your-own-index basis in Street Euro (ES) and Heads-up in Pro Euro (EP).

Ron Bartlett. V6 Ford Capri. 3100 cc — Insanity.

David Ward. Ferrari 308 GTA. 3000 cc Ferrari V8.

Keith Ridley. Reliant Scimitar. 3100 cc.

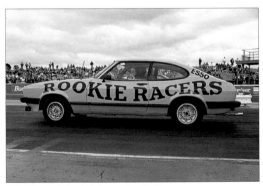

Mike Ellis. Ford Capri. 2000 cc — Rookie Racers.

Modified ET (Mod ET)

10.00-11.49 Seconds.

Open to cars as per Street ET and Super ET, with or without wings and fenders, as well as dragsters or roadsters. The latter two types must have a body or a cowl of flameproof material extending beyond the firewall. The minimum wheelbase is 90 inches unless the car has the original engine – the minimum for dragsters is 125 inches. A roll cage is mandatory as is a five-point safety harness. The engine should be of automobile type. It may be relocated and can use either petrol or alcohol. Flywheel shields and aftermarket harmonic balancers are mandatory. Rev limiters and data recorders are allowed, but no other electronic devices. A minimum single layer fire suit is required.

Tony Guy. 1932 Model B Ford. 355 ci.

Lee Huxley. '32 Roadster. 460 ci.

Simon Hall. 1932 Model 'B'. 460 ci.

Paul Harvey. Dragster. 351 ci — Loco-Motion.

Martin Holgate. Comp Altered. 3800 cc — The Alcoholic Cat.

Twin Bikes

Most bikers have owned, or at least ridden, a twin at some time. A lot of them still do! And they want to race them competitively, not just look at the back of 'Johnny Buzzbox' as he approaches Mach One and disappears over the horizon.

With the introduction of the four and six cylindered 'Kawayamahondzuki' — miniature intercontinental ballistic missiles — the popular and possibly more traditional section of motorcycling, 'the big twin' became unfashionable and increasingly less competitive on the track and on the street (unless you had access to the original 'street yob bike', the RD250/350LC!). In 1993, the National Association of Supertwins (NAST) was founded as an independent club to help these people realise their dreams. With its sights set firmly on the protection and promotion of drag racing for the twin-cylinder motorcycle in the UK, the association runs four classes — these being Street (STS), Modified (STM), Top Gas (STG) and Top Fuel (STF).

Russell Reeves. Triumph Bonneville. 850 cc.

Tim Clarke. Nourish. 900 cc.

Darren Boulstridge. Yamaha RD400DX. 430 cc.

Adam Hewitt. Harley Davidson. 140 ci.

Rover V8 Challenge

The Rover V8 Challenge has been around since the early eighties. It was originally Sponsored by John Wolf Racing and Street Machine but, for most of its history, by the current class sponsors Real Steel, and Custom Car. Around 1990 the Rover V8 Drag Race Association (RVDRA) was formed to run the Rover V8 Challenge and it is now a fully RAC recognised club. The class was the first of its kind. It is unique in so far as it allows only the British Rover V8 as the power unit. As it grew, it was split into two; Street and Pro. The difference is that Street Rovers are confined to Street tyres (the most limiting factor on a drag car). There is to be a third class added for 1996, giving Street (SR., 4.0L, Street tyres only), Super Street (SSR., 5.0L, any tyres), and Pro (PR., as Pro now). Details will be decided during the winter recess. Potential new competitors should contact the RVDRA. In practice all of the really competitive cars in Pro have full tube chassis, etc and are effectively just like Small Block Pro Mods. Great fun to watch!

Steve Law. Ford Escort Mk I. 3900 cc.

Ian Hampstead. Ford Escort Mk I. 4500 cc.

Phil Eaves. TR7 V8. 4700 cc.

Paula Atkin. Ford Escort Popular 100E. 4500 cc.

Super Gas (SG)

9.90 Index.

This is run to an index of 9.90 seconds and is one of the most closely contested classes on the UK scene. It is open to roadsters and full-bodied cars with windshield, operational doors and handles. They must use an original factory body or replica, but customising and/or tube frames are permitted. The car must have a maximum turning circle of 13 metres. Any automobile engine is accepted, which may be relocated and carburetted, injected, turbo- or supercharged — with either petrol, diesel or alcohol. It must have a fitted self starter, with two headlights and two tail lights in original positions. A five-point harness and two layer fire suit are required.

Throttle Stop

All of the front runners are capable of times quicker than 9.90. Many use a device known as a Throttle Stop to slow their time down to the index. For instance, if the car can run 9.50, but the day's temperature, air pressure and humidity are likely to slow that by a tenth to 9.60, the throttle stop timer will be set to delay their run by a further three tenths. It also means that the terminal speed is greater than would

be the norm for a 9.90 car, which can be handy to catch your opponent just before the finish. But the driver still has to get away from the line first. Remember, it is the first to the finish who wins, without running below 9.90 seconds.

Best Of British Super Gas

This event was supported by Terry Gibbs' Camaros Unlimited and Ashley Letts of Crane Cams. Twelve UK Super Gassers attended the Tenth Hockenheim Nitro Olympics in August 1995 and dominated their class, taking eight out of the top ten places. Some of their opposition didn't turn up if drawn against a British driver. Apparently we take it too seriously. They all put on a superb show for the huge crowd and were a great credit to UK drag racing. But be sure, with the ease of access the EEC has made for foreign competitors at UK National events, a lot of visitors will be seeking revenge in the future.

During 1995, proposals were made for a Super Competition class, to be run as Super Gas, but to an 8.90 second index.

Allen Flavell. Ford Pop — Fatal Attraction.

Paul Watson. '72 Dodge Dart. 440 ci Chrysler — Grumpy's Dodge.

Pro Stock Bike (PS)

Pro Stock is a petrol-burning class that seems to receive more media attention in the States, because of it's professional status there, than any other bike class. No turbo-charging, no super-charging or pumped fuel injection is permitted. All the main body parts must be stock or of stock appearance. A single engine must be used and it must be of a type that was specifically designed and manufactured for a production motorcycle. The engine manufacture will determine the make of the bike. Modifications to the engine are allowed provided they do not affect the external appearance of the castings. Original equipment manufacture (OEM) electronic fuel injection is allowed with unlimited modifications provided the injector bodies are of OEM equipment. The chassis must be based on a generally-available road-going frame, allowing a minimum ground clearance of 50mm, a minimum seat height of 500mm and a maximum wheelbase of 1778mm. Wheelie bars may be fitted with a maximum length of 3302mm from the centre of the front axle to the wheelie bar axle. There are a series of weight breaks for different engine sizes and set-ups.

Ray Debben. Kawasaki ZX10. 1428 cc.

Stefan Meserwell. Suzuki GSXR. 1260 cc.

Nigel Dowding. Yamaha FZR1000EXUP. 1098 cc.

Graham Dance. Suzuki 1100FJ. 1294 cc.

Dave Beck. Suzuki GSXR1100 with 1260 cc engine.

Steve Woollatt. PBR Puma. 1327 cc — Top Fuel bike, The Dealer — gets fired-up ready for a run.

The Wild Bunch

At the moment only general rules exist. A new class for the '96 season is intended for Nostalgia cars — typically old dragsters, altereds and slingshots. Altered describes a very custom or modified car based on a known style eg 'Ford Model T Altered'. Slingshot is the old dragster style where the driver sits right at the back, over the diff. Before the rear engine layout was developed all dragsters were built this way. It is basically an index class. Each competitor chooses his ideal time and multiplies it by four. He then has four heads-up passes to get a total time as near as possible to that figure. The event winner is the one who gets closest to his ideal time, as a percentage. Because all rounds are heads-up, they look like races to the spectator, even if he is unaware of the indexing. A red light will add a 10% time penalty for that round only. If one round is faster than expected, slow down on the next; there is no break out. There are some 60 entrants who have expressed an interest in this new class. Many are old cars, once retired from racing and seeking a new lease of life. Others are altereds from other classes. If new regulations, currently under discussion, outlaw altereds from even British Top Alcohol, this is the obvious class to attract them.

Rob Emmett. 1923 Ford Model T Altered. 427 ci — Yorkshire T.

Roy Wilding. Slingshot Dragster. 430 ci Buick.

John Guthrie. '23 Ford Model T Turtledeck. 3500 cc Rover — Quiet Riot.

Chris Hartnell, Slingshot Dragster. 400 ci Chevy.

Pro ET

*John Menetrier
on his first year
drag racing:
"it's been a blast".*

8.49-9.99 Seconds.

The next most serious class beyond Mod ET for those who break the ten second barrier.

Rules are as for Mod ET, except that nitromethane is allowed and a minimum double layer fire suit is required, with boots and gloves.

The class sees the appearance of a higher proportion of Dragsters and Altereds. All the ET classes are fiercely competitive at the top level. To be competitive you need consistency. These people call missing their dial-in by a tenth -of-a-second inconsistent.

Steve Warner. Dragster. 355 ci Chevy.

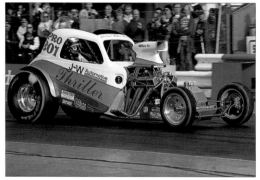

Richard Walters. 1976 Fiat Topolino Altered. 400 ci Chevy.

Ray Barrow. Chevrolet Vega. 355 ci.

Dave/Roger Moore. Triumph Herald. 400 ci Pontiac — Shaken not Stirred.

Chris Worsell. Dragster. 468 ci.

Super Pro ET (SP ET)

7.00-8.48 Seconds.

Rules are as for Mod ET, except that injected Nitromethane is allowed and a minimum double-layer fire-suit is required, with boots and gloves.

In practice, major competitors all run Dragsters to prove competitive. Regular visitors from the continent appear in Altereds and Wild doorslammers; steel bodied cars running down almost into Pro Modified times.

There are proposals to drop the lower ET class limit to six seconds to encourage greater competition.

Fay Fischer. Dragster. 515 ci Chevy.

Mick Kemp. Dragster. 500 ci KB.

Bertrand Dubet. '23T Altered. 477 ci (alcohol).

Martin Jones. Dragster. 482 ci Chevy.

Barry Giles. Dragster. 482 ci Chevy.

Outlaw Anglia races are always unpredictable, their burnouts even more so. The fire marshall in the distance took some rapid evasive action as the car approached him, then gave the driver a very old fashioned look.

Outlaw Anglias (OA)

Possibly the most unlikely race car, the Ford Anglias (or Pops) present the crowd with some of the best entertainment on the track. As far as we can gather, the only rules are that the car should look like a Pop with a <101 inch wheelbase, have side-by-side seating and no flip-up funny car style bodies. With around 1000 bhp from some of these little machines, wild start-line antics are a certainty. The cars look superb, the racing is furious; any event featuring Outlaw Anglias is guaranteed to be a good show.

Paul Hensher. Ford Pop. 498 ci B1 — Gas Attack.

Tony Baker. Ford Pop. 540 ci — Torque of the Devil.

Paul Wright. Ford Pop. 383 ci Chevy.

Cliff Griffin. Ford Pop. 350 ci.

Frank Griffin. Ford Pop. 392 ci Hemy.

Peter Bossert. Suzuki GSX-1150 EF. 1325 cc. Funnybike - Orient Express.

Neil Midgley. Suzuki GSX-1100 F. 1325 cc. Funnybike.

Funny Bike (FB)

Once combined with the Competition Bike class, Funny Bikes made a welcome return to a class of their own in 1995. The class is open to single engined, Nitro, alcohol, or petrol burning motorcycles. The rules and regulations for the class are similar to Competition Bike, but with a few specific exceptions. The entire bike must resemble the stock appearance of the bike it is based on, including front and rear mudguards. Forced induction motors may use alcohol or gasoline, with or without nitrous, but no Nitro. Normally aspirated motors may use alcohol or gasoline, with or without nitrous, or Nitro. Likewise, pushrod motors, whether forced induction or normally aspirated, may run up to 100% Nitro or with alcohol, gasoline and Nitrous Oxide.

Augy Harrison. Suzuki GSX1100EFE. 1260 cc.

Tim Blakemore. Kawasaki. 1260 cc.

Jean Yves Vetsch. Suzuki Katana. 1325 cc.

Chris Hampson. Suzuki. 1260 cc.

Barry Eastman. Honda CBX — Tokyo Express.

Pro Modified (Pro)

These are the fastest gasoline-powered cars in drag racing. Although alcohol is permitted within the class regs, a weight penalty means drivers choose not to use it. They have monster engines, over 1,000bhp, and are a fabulous spectacle to watch, with huge burnouts and 200mph, seven second races. The class grew out of the British Pro Stock class that ended in the 1970's. It is open to full bodied cars (doorslammers) with original factory body or replica. They must have at least two opening doors with operating handles, for exit either side of the car and road legal mudguards over all wheels. Wheelbase is to be between 99 and 115 inches and within 5 inches from the factory original. Extensive customising is permitted, but the rear spoiler must not be over 24 inches long and wheelie bars not over 104 inches. The engine must not be over 715 ci (11.716 litres) and must be self starting. Nitrous oxide is permitted and fuel may be petrol or methanol. Performance is such that most use Funny Car type wheels and tyres. There are minimum weight breaks, dependant on the engine size and fuel choice, but these are gradually being increased over the next couple of seasons to bring the UK Pro Modified class more in line with its US counterpart. Most cars competing in the class have been built by Robinson Race Cars and Andy Robinson will be returning to the fray for 1996 in a Rover 800.

A Pro Modified Run

Although there will undoubtedly be differences between each driver's technique, a typical Pro Mod Burnout and Run may be something like this. Having got the car started, pull forward into the Burnout box to wet the tyres and roll towards the start. Pull third and fourth gears together, apply a little line lock, balance throttle and clutch to get the tyres spinning and quickly grab second gear. The objective is to obtain maximum tyre revs with minimum engine revs. Release line lock to give a rolling burnout. Stop and reverse back behind the start line, holding the roof escape hatch open to let the tyre smoke out. Move forward into stage, using a little line lock pressure, and a balance of throttle and clutch. Purge the Nitrous, switch on the data logger, edge into pre-stage, nail the line lock and jiggle into full stage. Clutch to the floor operates the two-step rev controller to the launch setting — when the centrifugal clutch is released it will lock up fully in around seven seconds. When both cars are fully staged, floor the throttle. The engine will rev to the limiter setting (4-5000rpm) and sound as rough as a bag of spanners. On the lights, release the clutch and the line lock and watch your shift lights. Under one second and you grab second gear; probably still with the front wheels up. About one second later, switch the Nitrous to the second stage, watch your shift light again for third and fourth and get ready on the 'chute. Through the finish trap, pull the 'chute and the clutch down and kill the ignition (frequently done with the throttle open so that the plugs can be read). Oh… and I hope you didn't forget to steer with your other hand! A Pro Mod driver works for his six second adrenaline fix.

Dave Mingay. Vauxhall Calibra. 613 ci — Hellraiser IV.

Gordon Appleton. '67 Camaro. 665 ci — The Final Demand.

Competition Bike (CB)

Competition Bike is the start of the nearly-anything-goes classes. This class allows the competitor and/or bike builder to do/create almost anything they like. They can run a multi engined bike, use almost any type of fuel (except Hydrazine), fit a super-charger and use any type of frame. There are a number of rules that the competitor must comply with. A lanyard-operated, spring-loaded fuel shut-off valve is mandatory. It must be situated on the entry side of the barrel valve. Where Nitromethane is used a fuel shut off, which completely shuts off the fuel supply by a handlebar mounted control, must be provided. Drive chains and belts must be adequately guarded, by a 1/8 inch steel shield or equivalent, to prevent it touching the rider at any point. A minimum of 75mm ground clearance is recommended. Dual, twin-calliper front discs, with cylinders and lines adequately protected against accidental damage, are mandatory.

Jerry Collier. Yamaha RD400. 430 cc.

Ken Thorn. Kawasaki. 1170 cc.

Robert Brookes. Kawasaki. 1327 cc.

Andy Folberth. Kawasaki. 1260 cc.

Top Alcohol Funny Car (TA/FC) Top Alcohol Dragster (TA/D)

Zero to 100mph in under a second, the quarter-mile in six seconds and top speeds in excess of 230mph are typical.

Top Alcohol is a class originally introduced at the request of drivers because of the cost of fuel and the attrition rate associated with Nitromethane. The cars and engines are very similar to their Nitro powered cousins except that they use three-speed Lenco transmissions. Their 2,000-3,500bhp engines enable them to launch harder and to achieve quarter-mile times almost as fast as the Nitro cars. Performance figures of 0-100 in under one second, the quarter-mile in around six seconds, and top speeds in excess of 230mph are typical for the front-runners. Dragsters and Funny Cars compete against each other for the National and European Championships. This makes for large fields and gives the class great popularity. The majority of rules for Top Alcohol classes are the same as for Top Fuel, except that there are a series of minimum weight breaks, dependant on engine size. Dragsters are limited to 500 ci (8.2 litres), and Funny cars to 565 ci (9.25 litres) to keep performances similar and hence ensure close racing. Cars and drivers are weighed after each run in top level competition and capacity checking is undertaken by scrutineers. Some of the 1996 regulations may be changing, with the intention of eventual harmonisation of the classes world-wide. Older cars and Altereds are already ineligible for European competition. Unfortunately the changes may lead to such teams, or those with lower budgets that are not able to operate totally with fully certificated parts, being forced out of UK competition.

Anita Makela. 1991 Dragster. 438 ci JPI.

Micke Kagered. '94 Ford Mustang. 542 ci KB.

Barry Sheavilles. 1993 Hauser Dragster. 432 ci. Stagecoach VI.

Top Fuel Bike (TF)

This is the class for the ultimate drag racing bike. With a unique and distinctive sound. They are the two wheeled cousins of the Top Fuel Dragster from their supercharged Nitro engines.

They are stunning to watch, accelerating from 0-100mph in less than one second and 200mph in about six seconds. At night the headers spout big flames as the riders fly into the darkness beyond the strip. These bikes have to be seen running the quarter-mile.

Do not miss them.

Steve Woollatt. PBR Puma. 1327 cc — The Dealer.

Eric Tebuul. 1510cc.

Jules Boag. Puma Yamaha FJ. 1200cc.

Peter Svensson. 1700cc.

Henk Geeve. 1600cc.

AFC Funny Car

A Funny Car should have a Coupe or Saloon body contour that is based on a production style and a 100-125 inch wheelbase. In practice the profiles, although meeting the letter of the rules, have become rather stylised for aerodynamic reasons, the result being that it is difficult to tell them apart and even more so to recognise the parent body style. In general they have a 125 inch wheelbase tubular frame, with the driver seated between the rear wheels, and a Fibreglass or Carbon Fibre body. Minimum weight (including driver) is 2,225 lbs (1,009kg). The body is attached to the frame at the front and hinged at the rear, with a hinged escape hatch in the roof. This can often be seen after the burnout, when it is frequently opened as the car is reversed back to the line, so that the tyre smoke can escape. An Altered shares the same frame and engine, but has a different body shape; it is less aerodynamic and hence slower, less predictable and usually makes for an interesting ride! Funny cars (in contrast with their alcohol TAFC cousins) share the same monstrous Nitro burning engines as Top Fuel Dragsters. The engine must not exceed 500 ci and must not have an electronically controlled fuel injection. A fire retardant 'lower engine ballistic restraint device' must be used. Nicknamed the diaper. This is to catch the bits when the engine blows up, as are the supercharger, clutch and transmission blankets. Two parachutes are required, with separate releases, and fireproof shroud lines from the mount to the pack. A minimum five-point harness is required, along with arm restraints. Really serious fire suits are needed, with protective underwear (fireproof, not what you thought, although it makes a lot of sense), boots, gloves, balaclava, etc. This is because the driver sits behind the bomb in a Funny Car. In a dragster the slipstream pushes the fire away behind him.

The Cannonball

This is a special race for Funny Cars. It is unique in that both Alcohol and Nitro Funny cars compete side by side. It is a race of consistency, run over a total of a mile. Each car does three runs against the clock. Although these are not races per se, two cars usually run side by side. Each team adds up its three times and the two with the fastest total go into the final. The final is run heads-up; the first to the finish wins. So why both alcohol and Nitro cars? The alcohol cars launch harder, by virtue of their lower initial gearing. In general they are more reliable then Nitro cars, typically putting in a series of runs in the low sixes. The fuellers on the other hand have slower 60 foot times but higher top speeds. On a good run they are capable of runs in the mid-fives, but to win they have to have three good runs.

Gary Page. Dodge Daytona. 500 ci KB.

John Spuffard. 1994 Pontiac Formula Trans-Am. 500 ci JPi.

Top Fuel Dragster (TF)

If it goes round fast it might blow-up and shower the crowd with hot, spare parts. Therefore, it must be wrapped in a flak-jacket.

This is it. This is the class others merely aspire to. It is reserved for Nitromethane burning dragsters; vehicles built specifically for all out drag racing competitions, with a minimum weight (including driver) of 1,975 lbs (895 kg). The chassis has a minimum length of 180 inches, but in practice all are around the maximum of 300 inches. The engine must not exceed 500 ci and must not have electronically controlled fuel injection. The final drive ratio is limited to 3.2:1 and the tyres a maximum of 36 inches diameter, 114 inches circumference and 17 inches wide. Like funny cars, a fire-retardant lower engine ballistic restraint device must be used, together with a supercharger, clutch and transmission blanket. If it goes round fast it might blow-up and shower the crowd with hot, spare parts. Therefore, it must be wrapped in a flak-jacket. Two parachutes with separate releases and fireproof shroud lines from the mount to the pack are required. Serious fire suits, protective underwear, boots, gloves and balaclava must be worn. A minimum five-point harness and arm restraints are required.

Jens Nybo. 1991 ABC. 500 ci KB.

Rico Anthes. 1993 Swindahl. 498ci KB. Andy Carter in the background.

Tony Bryntesson. 1994 Brad Hadman. 500 ci KB.

Viveca Averstedt. 1995 Swindahl. 500 ci TFX-KB.

A Run in a Top Fuel Dragster

The clutch is gripping harder, the acceleration is pulling 4G and your field of vision has narrowed to a tunnel because of the force.

Rico Anthes.

A Top Fuel engine will run with either Gasoline, Alcohol or Nitromethane. The engines are always started using gasoline. With the fuel system off, ordinary petrol is squirted into the injector butterflies, and the starter engaged. When the engine fires, the crew chief stops squirting the petrol and the driver turns on the fuel.

In the pits, the engine is started and idled first time with alcohol in the fuel system. It idles evenly, smoothly. This enables the valve train, gear linkage, fuel system, etc. to be checked out after a rebuild, without using the £30 a gallon Nitro, and without yet exposing the engine to its corrosive effects. The fuel system has two settings, low and high. With the fuel pumps pumping at 200psi and up to six pints a second, the low setting returns most of it to the tank. High doesn't.

Just before the car is brought out for a run, it will be started again, but this time with Nitro in the tank. The even note of the alcohol is replaced by an evil, uneven crackle. Nitro. The engine will be allowed to warm up, so that the valve clearances can be set. A crowd will gather, drawn by the noise. Fingers in ears, they push to see what is happening, jostling for place. One by one they are beaten back, eyes streaming tears from the acrid fumes, their place to be taken by others. The canopy over the car will shudder and twitch as the explosive exhaust pulses beat against it. When the throttle is blipped, the revs and noise rise and fall so fast that all jump. The smell of burnt Nitro hangs heavy in the air. Tension rises.

When the engine is warm, the fuel is turned-off. The crackle of Nitro exhaust dies, the engine note evens out, rises slightly and falls to nothing. The crowd drift away, some talking animatedly, many stunned. Adrenaline does that.

The oil will be drained, checked and discarded. It is checked for any metallic debris that would indicate a potential failure, and discarded as it is now contaminated by the corrosive Fuel. Then new oil is added, and the car towed to the staging lane. With the Gladiators ready, battle can commence.

Exact routines and cockpit layouts vary, but may be something like this. You are fully suited. Your underwear, suit and shoes are all designed to protect you against fire. You've got your earplugs in. Once in the cockpit, the five straps are tightened by the crew. Acceleration is such that any free movement could result in injury. The gloves, arm restraints, helmet and the neck brace are fitted. The steering wheel is clipped into place.

A crewman is hand cranking the engine, slowly turning it so that fuel does not collect in the cylinders and fill one. That would cause an instant Hydraulic explosion when the engine was started.

Ready. The fuel lever is set high, the brake on, forward is selected, the clutch in. A nod passes between driver and crew chief. The crew chief squirts petrol into the injector and the starter is actuated. The engine fires and, as soon as its' note settles, you smoothly turn on the fuel. You watch the oil pressure dial to make sure that it rises to 100-120 lbs-per-square-inch. As the engine note settles down with the Nitro, you turn the fuel rate down low. At idle a lot of it is being blown out of the headers unburned.

When signalled forward by the crew chief you release the clutch and ease off the brake so that you move slowly through the water-box. Again on the signal you squeeze the throttle just a little to light up the tyres and then you do your burnout. As the clutch timing mechanism isn't actuated yet, the first blip of power locks the centrifugal clutch hard and the tyres spin.

The crowd are already on their feet, every last one of them. Those who know what to expect already have their fingers in their ears. The rest do soon enough. With six foot

Tommi Haapinen. The burn-out may roll the car forward too fast.

Andy Carter launches for a sub 0.9 second 60 foot time.

flames bursting from the headers, the wheels spin. Almost instantly the tyres grow a foot in height and the rear of the car leaps. Smoke pours from the tyres. The car rolls forward across the line, leaving two black, smoking lines of rubber from behind the line, to beyond the 60 foot mark. When you come off the throttle, the tyres collapse again. Still the car rolls-on, sometimes almost to the eighth mile.

Stop the car gently with the clutch and brake. Once again you check the oil pressure. You then select reverse and return to the start with the clutch and brake, making sure too much heat doesn't get into the clutch. Watch for crew signals which will guide you back exactly onto the still hot tyre-marks over the line. When signalled to do so, you stop, breath deeply and select forward. You ease the brake to creep forward. A crewman stands by the line, showing how far there is to go. Next, move into pre-stage and check the oil pressure for the third time.

Holding the brake hard, let the clutch out and simultaneously turn the fuel lever to the high side. Whereas before the engine note held a menacing crackle, now it drops a tone, becoming positively evil. There is so much fuel being forced into the engine that it actually cools-down rather than getting hotter. The car really wants to go so you ease off the brake slightly to let it roll the few inches to full stage. Three amber lights appear on the tree. Go.

You put your foot to the floor (0.26 seconds) and release the brake. (Although with the kind of power under your foot, no brake on earth is going to stop you.) The engine climbs to 7,000rpm in around a tenth of a second, the clutch starts to grip, the transmission turns the wheels, winding the tyres like springs (0.06 seconds). It takes the

required 0.4 seconds for the green light to appear. Your total reaction time was 0.42; almost perfect. The car moves, lifting the front wheels a couple of inches for the first 50-100 feet. The noise is so loud that the ground shakes.

The 60 feet comes up in 0.88 seconds; speed is already around 100mph. The clutch is gripping harder; acceleration is around 4G. The angle of view from your eyes has narrowed to a tunnel because of the force. The eighth mile at about 3.3 seconds, over 230mph. The clutch had engaged fully by two-and-a-half seconds, the engine dropped to around 5,700rpm in four seconds. Now it climbs back to 7,000, and beyond to 7,500. With final drive ratio and tyre size fixed, top speed is determined by rpm over the finishing line. four-and-a-half seconds. The finish-line flashes by. 4.985 seconds, 288mph. You've just run the first 'four' in Europe.

Come off the throttle, pull first one of the 'chutes (bang! 5G deceleration), then the other one. You checked the oil pressure as you did this, and turned off the fuel. Brake smoothly. As you draw to a halt, the emergency crew are following behind, having pulled out from their refuge 400 yards beyond the finish. You don't need them, but they were already moving, just in case.

By the time you've unstrapped and climbed out, someone with a radio will be on hand to tell you of your record time. Your support vehicle will be along shortly, as will the TV crew. Your team have done their bit, you've done yours, it's now time to reward your sponsors for their help. Afterwards you'll watch the interview and conclude that you were talking complete gibberish. Adrenaline does that too.

Viveca Aversted at the Quarter mile on her 1995 European record breaking 5.05 run.

Glossary

Alcohol (1)	Methanol when used as a fuel in an engine.
Alcohol (2)	What circulates in the veins of the authors after a very rainy and depressing race weekend. Mostly ethanol rather than methanol based, with hops and malted barley.
Altered	A car based on a known body type but changed or radically customised.
Blower	Supercharger. The Blower belt is the bit that connects the blower to the crankshaft pulley.
Bracket	The upper and lower ET index limits on a class.
Break-out	Running faster than the index in handicap racing.
Burn-out	Spinning the driving wheels before a run to clean and heat the tyres.
Christmas Tree	The traffic lights in front of the competitors on the start line. They are linked with and controlled by the timing computer and lights.
Chrom Moly	Chromium Molybdenum steel. A type of tubing used for race car chassis because of its strength.
Chute	Short for Parachute.
CI (Cubic Inch)	A measure of engine capacity. To convert cubic inches to cubic centimetres (cc) multiply by 16.4. ie 500 ci is around 8,200 cc.
Deep Stage	A racer is in deep stage when he rolls forward beyond full stage so that his front wheel only interrupts the stage beam and the pre-stage light goes out. The racer is nearer the finish, but dangerously close to a red light. In some classes, eg Super Gas, deep staging is illegal and gets a red light.
Dial-In	In handicap racing, the time which the driver believes is the most consistent time he can achieve.
Dialled-In	A car is said to be dialled-in when the crew and driver are happy that it will run consistently.
Doorslammer	A full bodied car with doors.
Dyno	Dynamometer. A machine for measuring the power produced by an engine under dynamic conditions.
Eliminations	Tournament style competition where two competitors race each other. The winner progresses to the next round, and the loser is eliminated.
ET	Elapsed Time. The total time (in seconds) taken to travel from the start line to the finish line.
Firewall	A metal barrier separating the engine of a car from the driver.
First or Worst	When both competitors foul, it is either the first to foul or the worst offence which determines the loser. If your opponent has red lit, you will not lose by running under your index. The final arbiter of the rules on the day will be the race director.
Foul	An infringement of a rule during a run. This may be pulling a red light, crossing a lane boundary line, or running under an index.
Headers	Exhaust tubing. If the exhaust is combined into a single pipe it is a manifold.
Heads Up	Non-handicap racing, where both competitors are started together.
Hemi	An engine in which the combustion chamber is hemispherical.
Hole Shot	An advantage gained by a quicker reacting driver who leaves the start line before his opponent.

IHRA	International Hot Rod Association.
In Pre-Stage	A racer is in pre-stage when his front wheel has interrupted the first light beam just before the start line. Full-stage is only inches ahead.
In Stage	A racer is in stage when his front wheels have interrupted both light beams at the start line. (See also deep-stage.)
Index	An elapsed time establishing the limit for a handicap class.
Light Up (Tyres)	To apply power too abruptly to the tyres and cause them to spin and smoke, instead of gripping the track.
N_2O	Chemical abbreviation for Nitrous Oxide.
NHRA	National Hot Rod Association (USA).
Nitro	Nitromethane. The ultimate drag racing fuel.
Nitrous	Nitrous Oxide. When injected with extra fuel into an engine gives added horsepower because it contains accessible oxygen.
OEM	Original Equipment Manufacture. Parts which were made and installed at the time the vehicle was originally built.
Pairing Lane	See staging lane.
Protest	A complaint filed against a competitor, which will be investigated by the race officials.
Qualifying	Before eliminations begin, racers must qualify. If a field is too large, only the fastest qualifiers will get through to eliminations. Championship points can be earned by qualifying Number one.
Reaction Time	The drivers reaction time is the time between the last amber light coming on and his front wheel leaving the stage light.
Red Light	Foul light on the christmas tree, triggered by leaving the line before the green light.
RPM	Revolutions per minute. Frequently abbreviated to `revs.'
RWYB	Run What You Brung. A non race session where anyone can try their steed on the track for a nominal sum.
Slick	Smooth tyres with no tread. This gives the maximum amount of rubber on the road.
Staging Lane	The designated area for competitors to assemble before they run. Sometimes known as Pairing Lane, where competitors are paired ready to compete.
Stock	Standard factory appearance.
Street Legal	A car or bike which could (or does) qualify for an MOT.
Supercharger	A compressor, driven from the crankshaft, which raises atmospheric pressure fed into the engine, resulting in added horsepower.
Terminal Speed	The speed through the finish line.
Trackbite	A kind of liquid rubber sprayed onto the track surface that provides for added grip when it dries.
Turbocharger	A compressor, driven by the exhaust, which raises atmospheric pressure fed into the engine, resulting in added horsepower.
Waterbox	The puddle behind the start line where drivers wet their tyres for the burnout.
Weight Transfer	Critical to traction. Vehicles are set up to provide a desired weight transfer to the rear wheels.
Wheelbase	The distance between the centres of the front and rear wheels.
Wheelie Bars	Bars which stick out the back of a vehicle to prevent excessive front wheel lift.

Useful Names & Addresses

Organisation/Club	Contact Name	Telephone/Fax
Santa Pod Raceway		01234 782828/ 01234 782818
Santa Pod Race Club (SPRC)	Sue Gandolphi	01234 782636
Avon Park Raceway (Long Marston)		01789 414119
Avon Park International Race Assoc. (APIRA)	Wendy Talbot	01968 788114
York Dragway		01422 843651
Pennine Drag Race Club (PDRC)	Marjorie Lyon	01405 812637
RAC Motor Sports Association		01753 681736 (Licencing ext 270)
RAC MSA Championship Coord	Graham Beckwith	01924 848623